Healthy Living from the Start:

A Health Curriculum for Grades K–3

Oak Meadow

Oak Meadow, Inc.
Post Office Box 1346
Brattleboro, Vermont 05302-1346
oakmeadow.com

Item #b000006
v.020419

Contents

Unit I: Physical Body

Unit II: Personal Safety

Unit III: Healthy Habits

Unit IV: Self-Esteem

Unit V: Self and Community

Unit VI: Whole Health

Introduction

Welcome to *Healthy Living from the Start*, a comprehensive health curriculum that provides the framework for teaching children about health and well-being. Developing healthy habits in the early grades can help children maintain a high level of wellness throughout their lives.

Developing healthy habits in the early grades can help children maintain a high level of wellness throughout their lives.

Designed with flexibility in mind, this book has a format that allows you to easily customize your health program for use with multiple grades or in a sequential manner from kindergarten through third grade. The course is divided into 36 lessons, one per week for an entire school year. Each lesson includes three activities to choose from for each grade level, giving you a wide range of options for exploring each topic. Activities usually can be completed in 15–30 minutes.

This course offers a hands-on, experiential approach to health and fitness with varied activities that encourage children to learn by doing, making the learning more relevant and memorable. The material is divided into six units:

I. Physical Body
II. Personal Safety
III. Healthy Habits
IV. Self-Esteem
V. Self and Community
VI. Whole Health

Reviews are placed at the end of each unit, every six weeks, to give you a chance to go over previous information or to go into more depth on a topic of interest to your child. A checklist is provided with each review and you are encouraged to check off activities as you do them. This will give you a good record of the health topics covered during the year, and it will tell you at a glance which activities are still waiting to be enjoyed in future months or years.

This book is written with parents in mind, particularly homeschooling parents, but the curriculum can easily be adapted by teachers in a group setting. Sometimes you'll notice that the instructions specify that you should do something, or ask your child to do something, but oftentimes

Let these lessons become a starting point for you and your child to seek answers and explore topics together.

the instructions will be written as though you and your child are the same person. This is because you are encouraged to do these exercises with your child to promote good habits and to demonstrate proper technique. Doing the activities together also gives you the opportunity to personalize topics and makes it easier for you to adapt activities for your own family or group of children.

You may be surprised to find how much you know about health and fitness, or you may discover that there are a lot of areas where you might want to expand your knowledge. This book assumes that you, as the teacher, have a general knowledge of many of these topics. However, don't be discouraged if you don't know the nutritional makeup of the foods you eat or what task the kidneys perform. Turn each new question into an opportunity to learn. Let these lessons become a starting point for you and your child to seek answers and explore topics together.

Please keep in mind that this information is not intended to diagnose or treat illness or injury. The lesson material is designed to introduce topics related to health that will give your child a point of reference and framework for understanding health and illness, injury care and prevention. None of these activities is meant to address, detect, or treat abusive or traumatic situations.

All of these activities provide an excellent opportunity for practical conversations around health-related topics, and these conversations can be done anywhere and anytime. Be on the lookout for ways to incorporate healthy activities and health knowledge into daily life. You may find the list of recommended reading found in the back of this book to be a helpful resource.

Above all, feel free to be creative and have fun! If an activity strikes your fancy, create variations on the theme. Use these lessons as a springboard for your own ideas. Imbue the activities with a sense of humor and playfulness whenever possible. Health is not just another subject to learn—it is the foundation for an energetic, productive, exuberant life.

Healthy Living from the Start can open the door for you and your children to experience together a lifestyle of health and wellness!

DISCLAIMER: None of the information, instruction, or activities in this book is intended to take the place of the advice and care of a qualified health care professional. If you have any questions about your health or your child's, please consult your health care provider.

Lesson 1 Growth and Development

This week you'll expand your child's body awareness into the realm of growth and development. Choose one or more of the activities below and enjoy exploring together the ways that bodies grow.

Kindergarten

From babyhood to now

❑ **Look how far I've come**

Time to pull out the baby photos and videos, and tell stories about when your child was a baby! Children love to hear about when they were young, particularly about when they couldn't do something (climb the stairs or say a person's name correctly, for example). This activity never gets old.

❑ **What can babies do?**

This activity can be especially fun if you have a baby in the house, or there is one among your friends. This can start as a semi-serious experiment: Can the baby talk? Can the baby walk? Can the baby move a toy from hand to hand? It can quickly escalate into a silly game: Can the baby climb a tree? Can the baby whistle? Can the baby pour a glass of milk? No doubt the baby will enjoy the attention as your child tries to "teach" him or her to whistle or read a book. Of course, your child will realize these are silly ideas, but in the meantime, your child will become more aware of all the things he or she can now do that weren't possible in younger years.

If you have a baby in the family, you might move this conversation in another direction:

What do babies need? This is a good chance to talk about body needs that don't change (the need for food and air, for instance) and those that do (the need for water or a toilet, for instance, neither or which babies need)

❏ **Stages of life**

Bring your child's attention to the many different ages and stages of growth and development revealed in the people around you. If you can, identify the following stages: infancy, toddlerhood, early childhood, childhood, preadolescence (tweens), adolescence (teens), young adulthood, adulthood, middle age, old age (elders). You can take the opportunity to not only talk about physical growth and development, but also about mental and emotional growth, and how the development of intellectual or creative capacities can change over time and with experience.

Use this space to jot down notes and ideas about the activities.

Grade 1
Ways we grow

❏ **Measure me!**

Children love to keep a growth chart, and if you haven't started one yet, this is a great time to do so. If you have been keeping track of your child's height on a chart, wall, or doorway, compare different heights at different ages. Find other ways to measure your child. How much does your child weigh? How long his or her hair and nails are? Measure foot length, finger length, arm length, head circumference, hand span, and anything else you can think of, talking all the while of how bodies grow in different ways. Include siblings and pets—measure everyone!

❏ **Giving a hand**

Comparing hand size is another way to bring your child's attention to how bodies grow and change. Get a large piece of paper and paint your child's hand with a bright color of nontoxic paint. Press the hand onto the paper and lift it carefully. Write your child's name next to the handprint. Next, have each person in the family make a handprint, using different colors, if possible. Label each handprint and compare hand sizes. If you are feeling adventurous, do the same thing with footprints. If you are visiting the beach, you can easily compare hand- and footprints in the wet sand. Another idea is to make wet handprints and footprints on the sidewalk to compare shapes and sizes.

❑ **How old? How young?**

Does short mean young? Does tall mean old? Here is a fun way to focus attention on the different rates of normal growth by finding people (ones you know or people in photos in magazines) who defy what may be a commonly held belief. Ask your child: Do you know someone shorter than you who is older than you? Do you know someone who is taller than you but younger? Can you tell people's ages by their height? By their hair or faces? By their voices? By the way they walk? This activity can easily flow into a conversation about presumptions and judgments and respect for differences.

Grade 2

Body differences and diversity

❑ **Wonderful world of differences**

This is a great activity for introducing the subject of ethnic diversity. It can be done while you are out and about (large gatherings often provide especially diverse groups of people), or at home using photos from books and magazines. Begin by looking for similarities: That woman has the same color hair as I do. That boy has glasses like mine. That librarian has curly hair like Dad. You and your child can take turns pointing out similarities. Next, begin to notice differences: That grocery clerk was much taller than me; the old woman at the post office walked with a limp. Model sensitivity and respect by saying something like, "Sometimes people don't like to talk about their bodies," or by making sure to speak quietly or out of earshot of others. Present this activity with a sense of wonder at the amazing diversity of humankind.

❑ **Growing my way**

Use animal books or videos to explore about how quickly animals learn to walk, run, hunt, swim, etc. Compare this to humans in general and then to individual human beings. This is a good way to introduce the topic of learning differences, medical conditions, and special needs,

and to point out that every individual grows and develops at his or her own pace.

❑ **Every shade of color**

Begin this activity by having your child place his or her arm next to every willing person (friends, family, and neighbors) to look at the differences in skin tone. Probably no two people, even within a single family, will have the exact same skin tone. Next, have your child use colored pencils to try to capture on paper the many different shades of skin tone seen during the experiment. This will work best if you have available a large selection of colored pencils or a set of colors that can easily blend with one another. Watercolor paints are also a good medium for this activity. This exercise can also be done with eye color and hair color.

Grade 3
Body changes

❑ **Growing pains**

Sometimes growing up is painful in more ways than one. Many children experience physical aches and pains as their bodies go through a growth spurt, but growing up can be painful in other ways as children become aware of leaving behind the carefree state of early childhood. Ask your child what things he or she misses about being little. Fitting comfortably on laps and being carried might be mentioned, for instance. Let your child know, "It's okay to sometimes want to go back to a time when you were carried if your legs got tired, or to when others took care of so many of your needs and you weren't expected to do anything." You might even let your child act out some babyish behavior (such as letting you feed him or her) or play with outgrown toys. After some time reliving this earlier time, you can begin to discuss the privileges and benefits of being older that your child now enjoys. Perhaps the child has recently outgrown having to use a booster seat in the car, or now has a later bedtime than before. End this exercise by looking at the new freedoms middle childhood brings.

❑ **I'm still me**

Instead of focusing on what has changed, this is a chance to talk about what has stayed the same. Have your child make a list of all the things he or she can think of that haven't changed in recent years. At the same time, you make a list of ways that your child has remained the same.

Don't look at one another's lists until you are finished. Your list might include things like eye color, love of french fries, sleeping with a certain stuffed animal, humming when drawing, etc. When your lists are complete, compare them. This activity can give your child a sense of security during a time when so many changes are happening physically, mentally, and emotionally.

- [ ] **Tweens and what to expect**

Big changes are on the horizon for the third grader, and it's helpful to provide a space for talking about feelings as well as imparting knowledge. This is a great time to provide a book about body changes during adolescence. Often tweens prefer to read privately about hormonal and physical changes that may make them feel self-conscious. See the resource section for titles (Karen Gravelle and Lynda Madaras have written excellent books for girls and boys), or ask friends, a librarian, or search online. This is also an excellent time to establish a routine for talking and checking in regularly, such as just before bedtime or while riding in the car.

Notes

Lesson

Body Awareness

In this lesson, you'll help your child explore the amazing human body. Choose one (or more) of the following activities to do this week.

Kindergarten

Body geography: Outside parts

❑ **What's this?**

This is a playful questioning game where you point to something on your body or your child's (say, your elbow or your heel) and ask your child, "What's this?" You can take turns, letting your child point to something and asking you its name. Start off easy, with well-known body parts, and then make it more challenging: scalp, gums, knuckle, sole of the foot, small of the back, etc. Change things up by asking, "What do you call this?" and point to the arch of the foot or the earlobe and see if your child can come up with the correct term. Have fun by naming body parts faster and faster and having your child scramble to touch them: wrist, cheekbone, ankle, chin, shin, temple, forearm, jaw, forehead, eyelashes. Switch places and have your child name body parts in quick succession while you react as fast as you can.

Your comfort level and your family's values will help you decide whether or not you want to include genitals in this game (easily done if you are playing it at bath time or while dressing). If you do include all external body parts, you may want to include both the common name your family uses (if any) and the correct anatomical term. Using correct terminology along with more familiar terms will help your child feel more comfortable and informed if an illness, injury, or doctor's office visit requires discussion about genitalia.

❏ **Body tracing**

Place a large piece of paper on the floor and have your child lie down on it. Draw an outline of your child's body in chalk or marker. Your child might want to draw clothes, hair, face, and other features on it. Cut out the body shape and tape it to the wall or door.

If you don't have a large piece of art paper (from an easel roll, for example) or butcher paper (often used as packing material in boxes), you can glue or tape together several pieces. You can also do this activity outside, drawing chalk outlines on the sidewalk or driveway (make sure to color them in!).

❏ **Animal friends**

Use your pet for this activity, or borrow a pet from a friend. Examine the animal's body to find ways it is similar to the human body. Can you find the knee or ankle? Are there finger or toe joints like ours? What does the animal's tongue look like? Next, look for ways the animal's body is different: ears, tail, neck, etc. This is a fun way to marvel at the diversity of body types and body mechanics, and to gain a greater appreciation for the human body. Make sure the pet is a willing participant and comfortable with this attention. This is a good time to teach your child to respect animals.

Grade 1

Body geography: Inside parts

❏ **Where is it?**

This activity asks children to point to internal organs, which is much more challenging than identifying external body parts. They might not know very many organs yet, but they can probably point to their heart (and put their ear to your chest to listen to your heartbeat for proof of its location) and lungs (you might have to explain that lungs are used for breathing). Experiment with taking big breaths with hands on your rib cage to feel the lungs working. See if your child can point to stomach, brain, throat, bones, and muscles, too. Feel free to add complexity according to your child's interest and knowledge: bladder, kidney, diaphragm, veins. You may want to combine this activity with the body tracing activity in the kindergarten section above so your child can relate these organs to the body map.

❑ **What does it do?**

The goal of this activity is to explore the basic purpose of different internal organs. Depending on your own knowledge, and your child's interest, you may want to do a little research beforehand to brush up on your anatomy and physiology. Here is a basic list to begin with:

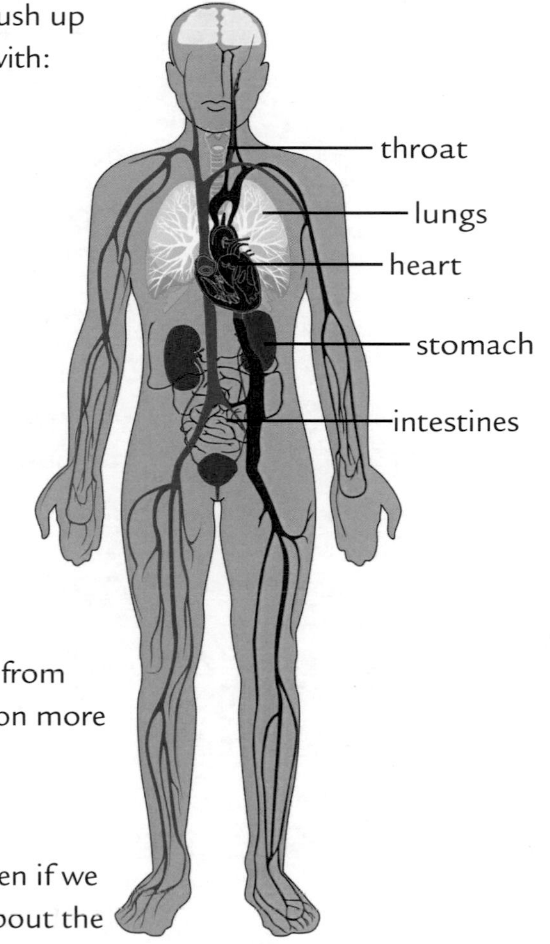

- heart: pumps blood through the body
- lungs: breathe air in and out
- throat: lets air into the lungs and food into the stomach—divided into esophagus (food) and trachea (air)
- stomach: digests food to give us energy
- intestines: absorbs nutrients from digested food
- brain: controls the body and houses all our thoughts
- muscles: move the body
- bones: support the body

Let your child try to feel where each body part is or get a book from the library with simple illustrations to help make the information more real.

❑ **I wonder...**

Sometimes asking questions can help us understand things, even if we don't know all the answers. The goal is to promote curiosity about the human body. You can search together to find the answers to any questions that really spark your child's interest. You might have to ask all the questions, or your child might be good at wondering about things. Here are a few questions to get you started:

- How many hairs are on your head?
- How long would your hair grow if you never cut it?
- What is the fastest a person has ever run?
- How long can a person hold their breath under water?
- How many pounds of food does a person eat in one year?
- How tall will I grow?
- Why are there lines on my palm?

Rather than looking for scientific answers to these questions, you might explore them in a physical way. Count the number of hairs in one tiny section of your child's head. See how fast your child can run, and how fast you can run. Place a piece of cardboard in your palm to keep you from bending it (pretending the skin was stiff and those lines weren't there) and see how hard it is to do things.

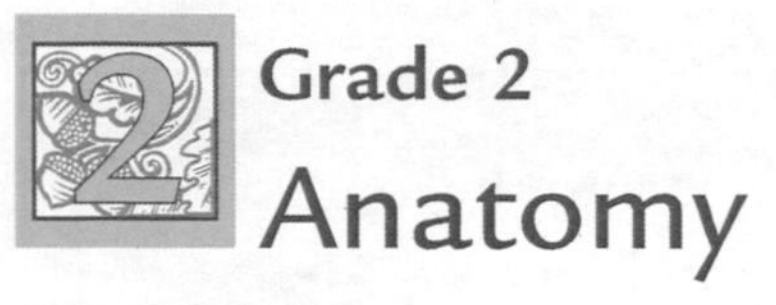

Grade 2
Anatomy

❑ **Amazing body**

Find a book in the library with a human body model and overlaid transparencies that allow you to see deeper into the body (skin, then muscle, then organs, then skeleton). Many encyclopedias have these, or you can search online. (You'll probably want to look for a good resource ahead of time since some are more graphic than others—a sketched version may be more appropriate than a photo-realistic one.)

If your child is interested, you can point out more complex body parts: esophagus, trachea, liver, kidney, intestines, etc. You can also trace a human body and have your child draw in organs or bones. *The Anatomy Coloring Book* is a wonderful resource, though it is aimed at high school and college students, so it is fairly complex. You can also find anatomy coloring templates online.

❑ **Making the connection**

This is a fun activity that is done standing up. Face one another and ask your child to move a single body part, such as a finger, without moving anything else. You do the same. The finger will be easy. Next, ask your child to move a hand or foot without moving anything else (and you do the same)—this gets a little harder and your child might notice other muscles or joints coming into play. Talk about what you are feeling and which body parts seem to be connected to others. Progress to more challenging tasks, moving ribs, neck, hips, etc., while trying to keep everything else still. It can't be done! You can't move your neck without moving your head; you can't move your hips without moving your knees, buttocks, or spine. Once you start laughing—which is very likely—talk about what moves when you laugh.

Skeletons

Explore the skeletons of animals and humans in as many different ways as you can. Here are just a few ideas:

- Find a skeleton model (check the doctor's office or a local university)
- View animal skeletons in a museum
- Examine animal skeletons found while out hiking
- View X-rays
- Play with Halloween decoration skeletons

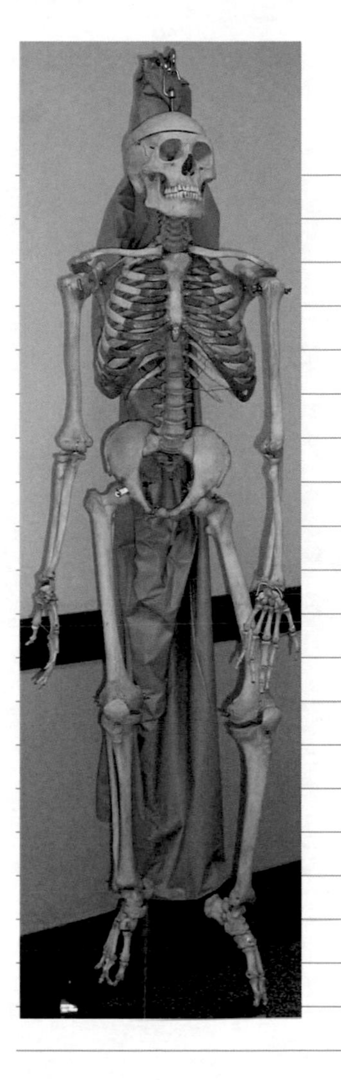

Make comparisons between your child's body (and your own body) and the skeletons, whether human or animal. If possible, explore how the bones and joints move. See how many moving parts (joints) you can identify. Some are obvious—knee and elbow—but what about jaw, spine, toes, etc.? If you can, name a few of the bones, or talk about how each one has its own unique name.

Grade 3

Privacy

Good touch, bad touch

This is an opportunity to talk about inappropriate touch in a very safe, empowering way. Depending on your circumstances and your child's personality, you can keep this information very general, or move carefully into the realm of abuse prevention. A good way to begin is to play a role playing game where you take turn touching each other's hand or arm in good ways and bad ways. For instance, a fingertip touch or a massage-type squeeze feels good, but a pinch or a slap doesn't. Experiment back and forth, taking turns, and talk about how everyone has a different threshold for pain and a different comfort level. Some people love deep massage, for instance, while others can't tolerate it, and some people love a light touch, but others are too ticklish.

You can stop the activity here, just discussing how to be aware of and respect the body sensitivities of others, or you can move the conversation into the realm of how some body parts are more public, so to speak, and others are more private. A good entry into this more serious conversation is to use the example of hugging. Talk about how a hug from someone you love makes you feel great but a hug from someone you don't like or don't know well can feel awkward or invasive.

❑ **Clothes, doors, and respect**

How does your family protect the privacy of each member? Who needs privacy and who doesn't? (Babies and dogs don't, for example.) What helps us be aware of the need for privacy and respect it? Each family has different rules and levels of comfort around privacy, nudity, and bodily functions. For instance, many young moms find it necessary to have the baby in the bathroom with them, but might prefer privacy from older children or other adults. This conversation can take place any time it naturally arises and be talked about when privacy needs change as a child gets older or as parents draw new boundaries.

❑ **Comfort zones**

What is a comfort zone? Does everyone have the same "zone"? Everyone has a certain comfort level with touch, privacy, nudity, etc., and even within a single family with shared values, individuals can feel very differently. As children grow toward adolescence, their feelings will undoubtedly go through a change in this regard, as well. For instance, young children usually don't pay any attention when their parents kiss, but older children often become uncomfortable or embarrassed by public displays of affection (even if these "public displays" take place inside the home!). Make space to discuss these matters with your third grader whenever a situation arises or whenever your child has questions or shows a natural change in a comfort zone level.

Lesson

Hygiene

Every child needs to learn how to properly care for his or her body. No doubt, your child has been learning by example since birth, but now you can begin to address specific topics in a more direct way.

Kindergarten

Keeping clean

❑ **Show me how**

Let your child show you how to wash hands, hair, and body, how to comb or brush hair (getting tangles out of long hair), and how to trim nails. Whatever he or she can't do yet, do for your child, showing tips to make it easier. Whatever he or she isn't quite doing correctly, gently show the correct way to make it easier. Another fun activity is having your child teach you how to do these things—washing hands, for instance. It can be fun to do exactly as your child says, taking all instructions literally. This may require patience from both parties! Even the simple act of washing hands takes more steps than you may think.

❑ **The skin you're in**

Fill a Ziploc plastic bag halfway with red-colored water or juice (cranberry juice works great). Pretend the bag is your body and the red liquid is the blood inside. If you'd like, you can add things to the inside of the "body"—edible things like fruit if you are using juice, or sticks, marbles, etc., if you are using colored water. These are the bones, muscles, and organs in the body. Explain that the bag is like your skin, which is like a big sealed envelope that keeps everything inside. Next, get a pin and a bowl, and let your child puncture the bag with a pin—a cut! Catch the "blood" in the bowl so it doesn't make a mess, or let it drip into the sink if you don't want to save it. As soon as the puncture is made, quickly try to seal the hole with a Band-Aid. This may or may not work, but it's a great way to begin talking about how your skin is self-sealing. A plastic bag will never "heal" from a cut, but your skin will. Discuss ways to take care of the largest organ in the body—your skin.

❏ **Getting dirty, getting clean**

Make a mud pit in the yard or dig in the garden until your child's hands are dirty. Have your child carefully wash hands (including under the nails) until they are completely clean. The dirt helps show whether your child is doing a thorough job with hand washing. Next, repeat this getting dirty/getting clean activity with feet. Depending on the weather, those who are really adventurous can do a full body roll in the mud and then hose off outside before getting in a hot tub and scrubbing head to toe. This simple, silly activity helps children not only practice practical washing skills but also appreciate the feeling of being clean.

Grade 1
Teeth

❏ **Be true to your teeth (or they'll be false to you)**

Let your child be the teacher and teach you how to brush and floss correctly. Exaggerate incorrect technique in silly ways (humor is always welcome) to focus your child's attention on the proper way to care for teeth.

❏ **Visiting the dentist**

If you can, visit the dentist's office to look at models of teeth, posters of dental health, and pamphlets of dental care. Speak to a hygienist, dental assistant, or dentist about any questions or anything you are curious about. You and your child can brainstorm a list of questions ahead of time. Here are a few possibilities:

- Why does plaque form on teeth?

- Are certain foods, snacks, or drinks particularly bad for teeth?
- Is eating fresh (raw) fruits and veggies good for your teeth?
- Why do baby teeth fall out?

❑ **Counting teeth**

This can be done with a hand-held mirror or just by feel. Have your child try to count his or her teeth—if that's too hard, you can do it for your child. Next, count your teeth. Do you both have the same number? Why or why not? Count the number of teeth of other family members and compare. Talk about how (and why) teeth change over time.

If you have a very docile and tolerant pet, count its teeth, too! Animal teeth are often quite different from human teeth in size, shape, and appearance. Look at what's different. Is anything similar?

Grade 2
Disease prevention

❑ **Rules to remember**

There are many things we do on a daily basis to stay healthy. Have your child create a list of health rules and illustrate or decorate it. Here are a few to get you started:

- Wash your hands before and after handling food and after using the bathroom. Wash hands when you arrive home after being outside or away from home (errands, visiting, etc.).
- Cough or sneeze into the inside of your elbow (not your hand) or into a tissue or handkerchief. Always turn away from others or from food when you have to cough or sneeze.
- Wipe or blow your nose with a tissue, and then throw it away and wash your hands. Don't use your shirt or hand to wipe your nose, and don't drop the tissue on the floor or table.
- Don't share drinks, food, or utensils when you or someone else is sick.

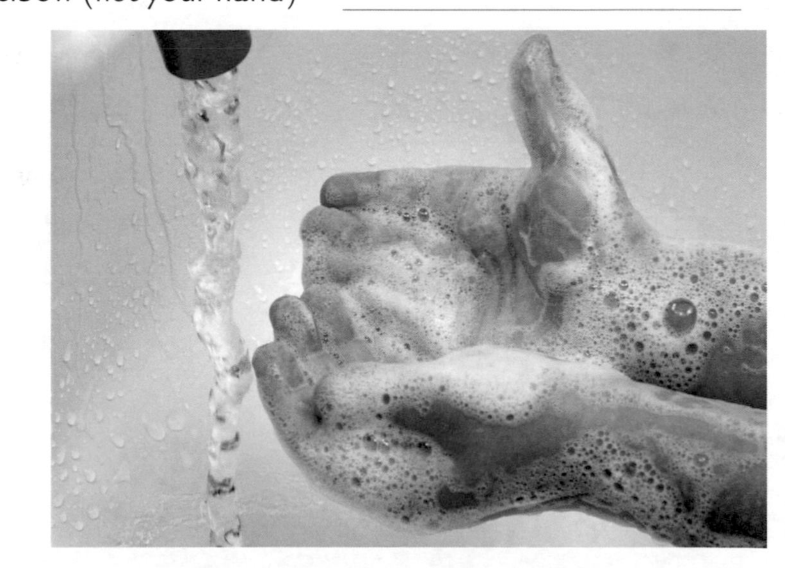

What other rules can you think of?

- [ ] **How things spread**

This activity is a bit messy (prepare for that!) but powerfully demonstrates how disease-causing germs can easily spread. Choose a brightly colored piece of chalk and color the palms of your child's hands. (Glitter is a great alternative to chalk for this activity; sprinkle some on each hand.) Next have your child spend five minutes doing normal activities in the house, such as opening doors and cupboards, picking up a glass or plate, pulling out a chair or touching your arm or hand. (For the sake of easy clean-up, you may want to limit this game to a single room in your home.) At the end of five minutes, have your child wash hands and then together see how many places you can find that are marked with chalk or glitter. Talk about how many illnesses are spread in this manner, and how washing hands can help stop the spread of the tiny germs that cause illness.

- [ ] **Building immunity**

In order to begin the conversation about building immunity or developing your resistance to illness, ask your child to list all the ways he or she can think of. Don't worry if nothing comes to mind at first. Begin a list together—this can be a list of words, or can be visual, with drawn illustrations or cut-out pictures. Include the following on your list:

- Eating healthy foods
- Getting plenty of water
- Getting enough sleep
- Being active and outdoors
- Washing hands regularly
- Having regular medical check-ups

Discuss why and how each item on the list helps build a healthy immune system.

Grade 3
Good grooming habits

❑ **Use your senses**

As adolescence nears, children sometimes don't realize when body odor begins to occur. Parents can be very aware of smells but may not know how to approach the conversation of body odor. This activity lets your child use sensory observations to guide grooming and hygienic behaviors. Begin by blindfolding your child and asking, "What do you smell?" After identifying household smells, ask you child to sniff his or her forearm and hand, and then describe the smells (if any). Next, sniff hair (have your child smell your hair if his or her hair is too short to smell), and finally have your child sniff his or her underarms. You can also sniff clothing to determine its freshness (including socks). This exercise is meant to bring awareness to body smells. Smells of soap, laundry detergent, shampoo, deodorant, or body lotion might be noticed during this exercise, although your child may not be able to pinpoint the source of the odor. Answering "it smells good" or "it smells stinky" is just fine. Conversations around the role of regular bathing and deodorant can follow, if necessary.

❑ **Long hair everywhere**

For children with long hair, keeping it neat and tangle-free can be a challenge. Spend some time experimenting with hairstyles—photos can inspire you or use your imagination. Children can learn to braid their own hair in different ways (one braid or two braids), and you can get more elaborate with French braids, Princess Leia braids, or a coronet-style hairstyle. Children can experiment with hair ties to keep their hair tidy. Experiment with hair gel for crazy hair style fun. Also, developing a nightly habit of brushing hair together can be very relaxing and make morning hair tidying quicker and easier.

❑ **Grooming checklist**

Brainstorm with your child a list of daily grooming habits and then create a chart together to post in a prominent place. It might include the following:

- brush teeth
- comb hair
- clean and trim nails

- clean wax out of ears
- wash hands and face
- wear clean clothes
- check appearance in the mirror before leaving the house

Add anything else you can think of that will help your child develop healthy grooming habits.

Lesson

Illness Prevention

Staying well is far preferable to getting sick and recuperating. Here are some activities around illness prevention.

Kindergarten

Staying healthy

❏ The big five

Play a game in which you and your child demonstrate or act out the five ways to stay healthy: eat healthy foods, drink plenty of water, get regular exercise and adequate sleep, and wash hands frequently. Pretend you have to act out these five activities in under a minute. Time yourselves! Too easy? Try to do it in under ten seconds. Another idea is to make up a song about how to stay healthy.

❏ Eyes, ears, nose, and mouth

Take turns being the doctor examining one another's eyes, ears, nose, and mouth. Use a flashlight to see better and make it seem more official. Pretend to find surprising things inside. Talk about what the doctor sees when you are sick.

❏ Water every day

Sometimes children (and adults) are so busy during the day that they forget to drink adequate amounts of fluids, especially water. Help your child chart how much water and other liquids are consumed in one day by each of you (or other members of the family). This is an exercise in awareness, but can also be a tool to increase fluid intake or to shift to drinking more water and fewer sweet drinks, if necessary.

Grade 1
Recognizing illness

❑ Body check-in

Knowing how you feel when you are well helps you recognize symptoms when you are sick. Have your child do the following and report his or her observations:

- feel forehead
- swallow
- look at own eyes
- take a deep breath
- focus on stomach sensations
- move arms and legs

Talk about how each of these body parts or sensations might change due to illness.

❑ What comes out

It's helpful to talk about the unpleasant aspects of illness: diarrhea, vomit, and mucus. No doubt your child has experienced these things but probably doesn't know why they happen. Talk about the body's instinctual efforts at righting itself. If you aren't sure why the body produces these reactions, do a little research on your own, or get a book from the library and read it together.

❑ Colds and flu

What's the difference between a cold and the flu? Both are respiratory illnesses (they affect your breathing systems) but they are caused by two different viruses. Colds and flu can produce the same symptoms, but usually the flu comes on very suddenly and makes you feel much worse than a cold does. Many people mistakenly call intestinal or stomach viruses the "stomach flu" but those illnesses, which produce nausea, vomiting, and diarrhea, are not caused by the influenza virus.

Here are some guidelines to share with your child to prepare yourselves for the next bout of the common cold or influenza:

COLD symptoms may include:

- runny nose
- watery eyes

- stuffed up nose
- sneezing
- coughing
- sore throat
- fatigue
- headache (from sinus congestion)

Treatments that might help:

- Drink plenty of fluids to help break up the mucus.
- Soothe a sore throat by drinking hot tea.
- Eat hot soup (if you eat meat, chicken soup is the preferred remedy); hot soup is easy on the throat and provides extra fluids.
- Use plenty of tissues and blow your nose often to get rid of mucus; remember to cover your mouth and nose with a tissue or with your elbow when sneezing or coughing.
- Stay warm (so the body can use all its energy to get well).
- Take a hot shower or stand in a steamy bathroom to help relieve congestion.
- Get extra rest during the day and more sleep at night.
- Wash hands and drinking glasses or water bottle to keep from infecting others or re-infecting yourself.

FLU symptoms may include:

- headache
- fever and chills (feeling hot and cold alternately)
- sore throat
- runny or stuffy nose
- body aches
- fatigue

Treatments that might help:

- Drink small sips of water; a bent straw in the cup makes drinking in bed easier.
- Suck on ice chips or ice pops to help stay hydrated.

- Use a cool, wet cloth on the forehead when feverish.
- Stay warm, adding an extra blanket to the bed.
- Use a warm washcloth to wipe skin if sweaty from fever, and change to dry clothes as necessary.
- Lie down, rest, and sleep as much as possible.
- Stay away from public places and wash your hands often to avoid spreading the illness.
- If a dry cough is present, a humidifier can help soothe the throat.

Grade 2

Being sick

Garden delights

Children love to grow things in a garden, flower pot, or window box. Here are some plants that have been used throughout the ages and are fun to grow.

- Mint: traditionally used for soothing an upset stomach. Make tea from dried leaves (see instructions on next page).
- Marjoram and sage: tasty in many cooked dishes, these herbs were commonly used to aid digestion.
- Aloe: the gelatinous sap inside the leaves helps heal and reduce the pain of burns. Cut open a leaf and spread the sap gently on burns or small cuts and scrapes.(Burns are first treated with cool water, but aloe is sometimes used once the pain is gone, and you are sure further medical attention is not needed.)
- Chamomile: traditionally used for soothing and calming anxiety or emotional upset—remember Peter Rabbit's mother giving him chamomile tea after his fright in Mr. McGregor's garden? Make tea from the dried flowers.
- Dandelion: the leaves are full of immune-boosting vitamin C. Eat the leaves fresh in salads or steam them.
- Lavender: often used to create a relaxing bath. Add dried flowers to hot bath water for a fragrant, soothing soak, or make tea from dried leaves and flowers.

To make tea:

Use one teaspoon of dried herb per one cup of boiling water. Steep for ten minutes and strain before drinking. Add honey to sweeten, if desired.

❑ **Warm comfort**

Sometimes a hot water bottle can comfort a child who is under the weather. Resting the hot water bottle on the tummy, back, or chest can be very soothing. (Take precautions when filling the hot water bottle and securing the top to safeguard against burns from boiling water.)

Help your child make a cozy, cheerful cover for your hot water bottle. Using an old sweater, tee-shirt, or flannel, cut two pieces large enough for it to fit into. Sew seams on three sides, and hem the fourth side (the opening where the hot water bottle will slip in).

❑ **TLC (Tender loving care)**

We all need TLC every day, but never more so than when we are sick. Have your child create a TLC card to have ready for the next time someone in the family is ill. This card will list all the things others will do to help the sick person feel better. Your TLC card might include the following:

- tea delivered to the bedside
- flowers in a vase
- box of tissues handy
- a picture or card to cheer up the sick
- promise of watching a movie together or keeping the home quiet

Grade 3
Contagious diseases

❑ **Fly through the air with the greatest of ease**

To demonstrate how airborne contagions travel, begin by having your child use a broom to vigorously sweep (indoors or out) and then use a flashlight or sunlight to watch the dust motes moving in the air stream. For an even more lively demonstration, turn on a table fan and drop tiny pieces of shredded cotton balls in front of it. Use these experiments

to talk about how some diseases are spread through airborne particles that are difficult to avoid, making immune-boosting healthy habits essential.

❑ **Keep it to yourself: bodily fluids and contagious illnesses**

Have your child list all the fluids that the human body produces. Once your child's list is complete, add to it as needed to expand your child's awareness and knowledge, explaining that all bodily fluids can transmit illness. The list should include saliva, mucus, vomit, blood, urine, and feces. You may or may not want to mention semen and vaginal fluids, depending on your child's knowledge, sophistication, and development.

There's no need to go into too much detail about illnesses being spread through bodily fluids (unless you have a reason to, such as a family member whose medical condition requires special precautions in the household). The point of this activity is to create an awareness of the body and the responsibility for everyone to do their best to keep from passing along illnesses.

❑ **Wise words**

There are many traditional sayings that have guided parents and healers for centuries. Some of these have thankfully fallen out of favor, but there are some sayings that are worth remembering. With modern science and the medical establishment backing them up, much traditional wisdom has proved its healing powers. Share these sayings with your child and talk about why they work or why they don't.

- **Feed a cold, starve a fever.** This popular saying is misleading because while someone with a fever may not feel like eating, you shouldn't intentionally starve them or force a fast. Whenever a body is sick, it needs a balanced nutritional diet. However, the grain of truth in this saying is that it is likely that someone with a cold will need to be encouraged to eat a hearty diet (not being able to smell food because of a stuffed up nose can decrease a person's appetite), and someone with a fever may not be interested in food, and that's okay, especially if he or she has the flu. Anyone with a fever should be encouraged to drink water to keep from getting dehydrated, and if possible, eat small amounts of bland foods.
- **Carrots improve your eyesight.** Carrots are full of Vitamin A, which is essential to healthy eyesight, so in that sense, this

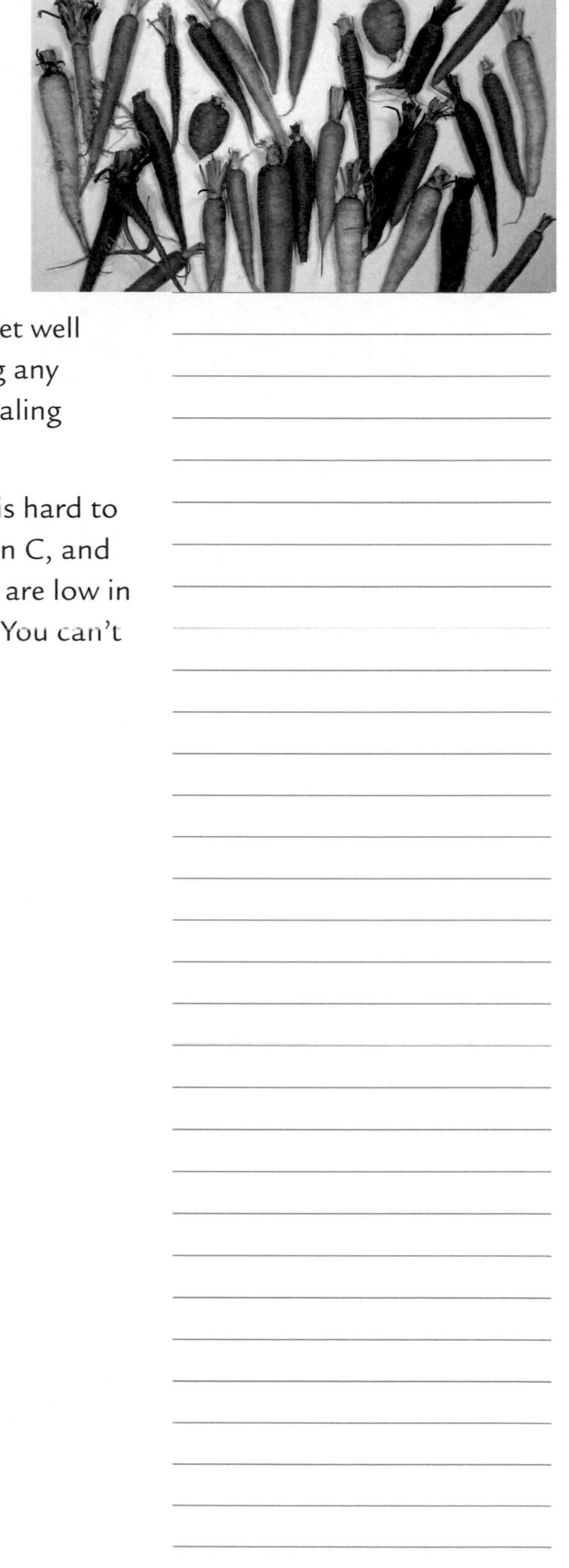

saying is true. But unless your eye problems are the result of a Vitamin A deficiency, carrots aren't going to help correct a vision problem.

- **Chicken soup cures a cold.** The curative powers of chicken soup (homemade, if possible, by someone who loves you—never underestimate the healing power of loving care!) are well-documented. While eating chicken soup is not going to instantly cure your cold, it can't hurt, and will probably help you get well faster. However, vegetarians need not despair: eating any healthy, warm soup will impart some of the same healing powers.
- **An apple a day keeps the doctor away**. This saying is hard to argue with. Apples are packed with nutrients, Vitamin C, and fiber—all of which are essential to good health. They are low in calories and readily available, too. The bottom line? You can't go wrong with an apple.

Notes

Lesson 5

Basic First Aid

It is a pretty good bet that everyone will find themselves in need of basic first aid skills at some point in their lives. Even young children can learn the basics. This knowledge gives children a foundation for injury care and may enable them to be more cooperative the next time they are injured.

Kindergarten

Cuts and scrapes, bumps and bruises

❑ **Band-Aid, ice, or heat? What does it need?**

While any serious injury needs to be cared for by a medical professional, many minor injuries are successfully treated at home with adhesive bandages (Band-Aids) ice packs, or a heating pad. Talk with your child about the purpose of each of these home care methods.

- Adhesive bandages: These are used for small cuts to help stop the bleeding by holding the edges of the cut together while the blood clots. Band-Aids also protect the cut from dirt and bacteria that may lead to infection.
- Ice: Ice packs are used to reduce swelling. It's important to make sure there is a layer of cloth between the ice and the ski so the skin doesn't get frozen. Ice packs can be used for 15–2 minutes at a time, giving the skin time to warm up again before reapplying the ice pack. Ice is particularly useful to control swelling soon after an injury occurs.

- Heat: Heat is used to soothe soreness, especially hours or days after the initial injury. Care should be taken that the heating pad is not too hot (especially when used for a child) or kept on too long (15–20 minutes should suffice). Heating pads should be turned off when not in use, and should not be used overnight or while sleeping. A hot water bottle or washcloth run under hot water and squeezed dry can be used in place of a heating pad.

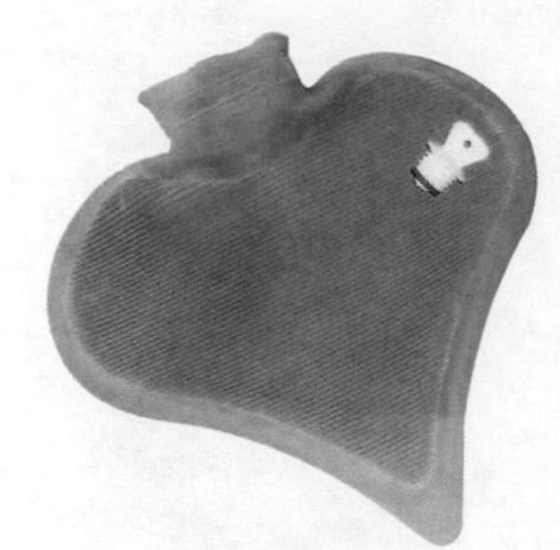

❑ **Caring for a cut**

Adhesive bandages (Band-Aids) are used when there is a small break in the skin that is bleeding. To care for small cuts, show your child how to follow these steps.

1. Wash hands before caring for the cut.
2. Gently wash away any dirt, blood, or debris from the cut.
3. Dry the cut with a clean cloth.
4. Open the Band-Aid without touching the white (sterile) cotton pad in the center.
5. If using an antibacterial agent (such as an antibacterial ointment), place a small amount directly onto the white sterile pad of the Band-Aid (not directly on the cut).
6. Place the Band-Aid carefully over the cut, sealing the bandage in place snugly (but not tight enough to restrict the blood supply).
7. Wash hands when you are finished.

❑ **Sew an ice pack cover**

Help your child make a soft cover for your ice pack. Using an old tee-shirt or cloth napkin, cut two pieces large enough to fit over the cold pack. Sew the seams on three sides, and hem the fourth side (the opening where the pack will slip in).

Grade 1
Caring for broken bones

❏ Wearing a splint

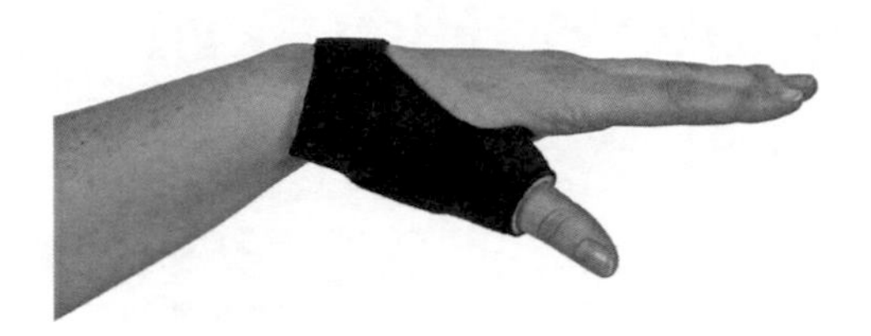

Sometimes an injury will be severe enough to require a splint, a rigid form that holds the injured body part in place. If you hurt a bone, you want to immobilize the joints on either end of the bone; if you hurt a joint, you want to immobilize the bones on either side of the joint. Have your child get a feel for what a splint does by creating and wearing one. Get a Popsicle stick, or cut a sturdy stick to finger length, and tear a few narrow strips of cloth. Have your child choose a finger to splint (or two to splint together, as is often the case to help keep the injured finger more immobile), and then place the splint on the inside of the finger so that it can't bend. Tie the splint in place with the strips (not too tight). See if your child can wear it for one hour. (Only trained professionals should splint actual injuries; this exercise is intended solely as a learning experience.)

❏ Making a sling

Slings are used when an injured body part (usually the arm, wris shoulder) needs to be rested and kept immobile. Use a large bar or square cloth to make a sling. Have your child pick an arm to p the sling. Fold the cloth in half to form a triangle, and place the of the triangle under the elbow. Bring the ends up and tie them t gether over your child's shoulder. Have your child wear the sling hour, if possible.

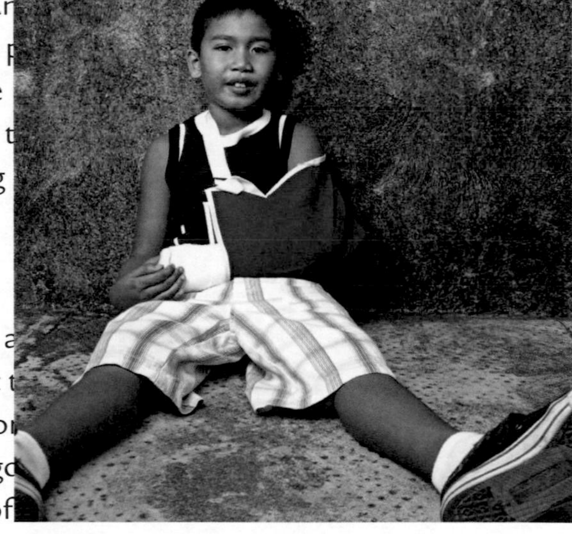

❏ Making a plaster cast

Broken bones often require a hard plaster cast to protect them a keep them immobile while healing. Help your child make a cast t experiment with what wearing a cast feels like. Blow up a balloo use as your cast form (an oblong shaped balloon will create a go arm-shaped cast). You can use either papier-mâché or plaster of Paris for this project—papier mâché is easier to work with but plaster makes a more authentic cast. Mix and apply the plaster cast to the balloon according to the directions, adding layers of newspaper or cloth strips so that you create a tube shape with two open ends. When the cast dries, pop and remove the balloon, and slip an arm inside. If possible, have your child wear the cast for one hour to see what it feels like.

Grade 2
Medical supplies and equipment

❑ **First aid kit**

If you have a first aid kit in the house or car, go over the contents of the kit with your child. Talk about the purpose of each item and how and when it is used. If you don't have a kit, consider creating one together.

❑ **Pharmacy visit**

Spend some time at your local pharmacy looking at and discussing the many medical supplies and equipment. Talk about the difference between a cane and a walker, for instance. Why would someone need tweezers for first aid? When, how, and why would you use a thermometer?

❑ **Ambulance exploration**

If you can arrange it, explore the inside of an ambulance and have an EMT explain some of the medical equipment. If you can't do this in person, find a book in the library or information and photos online.

Grade 3
Medical careers

❑ **Medical jobs**

Ask your child to list all the medical jobs he or she can think of, and then add your own ideas. The list might include the following jobs:

- paramedic
- surgeon
- chiropractor
- nurse
- phlebotomist
- surgeon
- emergency room doctor

- midwife
- X-ray technician
- anesthesiologist

You might also include acupuncturist, naturopath, homeopath, or other fields of natural medicine. Have your child choose one or two to learn about in more detail.

❑ **Medical specialties**

Ask your child to name a body part or system, and together find the title of that specialized area of medicine. There are some pretty impressive titles, and they are fun to say. Research as many as you like. Here are a few:

- bones: orthopedics
- heart: cardiology
- ear, nose, and throat (ENT): otolaryngology
- feet: podiatry
- stomach: gastroenterology

❑ **Ask the doc**

If possible, visit a doctor's office to chat with the doctor about his or her job. Brainstorm with your child a list of questions ahead of time, such as:

- What do you like best about your job?
- When did you decide to become a doctor? Why?
- What are some of the most challenging parts of your job?
- How long did you study to become a doctor?

Notes

Lesson 6 Unit I Review: Physical Body

Check off the activities you completed in the first unit (lessons 1–5). Review any information that your child was particularly interested in and take some time to explore the topic more fully, or revisit activities that your child especially enjoyed. Feel free to try one or two new activities to increase your child's knowledge of the physical body.

Lesson 1: Growth and Development

KINDERGARTEN	**From babyhood to now** ❏ Look how far I've come ❏ What can babies do? ❏ Stages of life
GRADE 1	**Ways we grow** ❏ Measure me! ❏ Giving a hand ❏ How old? How young?
GRADE 2	**Body differences and diversity** ❏ Wonderful world of differences ❏ Growing my way ❏ Every shade of color
GRADE 3	**Body changes** ❏ Growing pains ❏ I'm still me ❏ Tweens and what to expect

Lesson 2: Body Awareness

KINDERGARTEN	**Body geography: Outside parts** ❑ What's this? ❑ Body tracing ❑ Animal friends
GRADE 1	**Body geography: Inside parts** ❑ Where is it? ❑ What does it do? ❑ I wonder...
GRADE 2	**Anatomy** ❑ Amazing body ❑ Making the connection ❑ Skeletons
GRADE 3	**Privacy** ❑ Good touch, bad touch ❑ Clothes, doors, and respect ❑ Comfort zones

Lesson 3: Hygiene

KINDERGARTEN	**Keeping clean** ❑ Show me how ❑ The skin you're in ❑ Getting dirty, getting clean
GRADE 1	**Teeth** ❑ Be true to your teeth (or they'll be false to you) ❑ Visiting the dentist ❑ Counting teeth
GRADE 2	**Disease prevention** ❑ Rules to remember ❑ How things spread ❑ Building immunity
GRADE 3	**Good grooming habits** ❑ Use your senses ❑ Long hair everywhere ❑ Grooming checklist

Lesson 4: Illness Prevention

KINDERGARTEN	**Staying healthy** ❑ The big five ❑ Eyes, ears, nose, and mouth ❑ Water every day
GRADE 1	**Recognizing illness** ❑ Body check-in ❑ What comes out ❑ Colds and flu
GRADE 2	**Being sick** ❑ Garden delights ❑ Warm comfort ❑ TLC (Tender loving care)
GRADE 3	**Contagious diseases** ❑ Fly through the air with the greatest of ease ❑ Keep it to yourself: Bodily fluids and contagious illnesses ❑ Wise words

Lesson 5: Basic First Aid

KINDERGARTEN	**Cuts and scrapes, bumps and bruises** ❏ Band-Aid, ice, or heat? What does it need? ❏ Caring for a cut ❏ Sew an ice pack cover
GRADE 1	**Caring for broken bones** ❏ Wearing a splint ❏ Making a sling ❏ Making a plaster cast
GRADE 2	**Medical supplies and equipment** ❏ First aid kit ❏ Pharmacy visit ❏ Ambulance exploration
GRADE 3	**Medical careers** ❏ Medical jobs ❏ Medical specialties ❏ Ask the doc

Notes

Lesson

Personal Awareness

Being aware of your surroundings—the hazards as well as things that can be useful—and paying attention to people around you can help you stay safe wherever you are. In this lesson, you and your child will explore the basics of personal safety.

Kindergarten
Home safety

❑ **A safe home**

There are many safety measures and safety hazards in the home that children may know about but not understand. In this activity, you will take a tour of your house to find items related to safety and discuss their uses. Here are some questions to help you start a conversation, based on what you find in your home:

- Do you have a fire extinguisher? Where is it? Have you ever had to use it?
- Do you have smoke detectors and a carbon monoxide detector? Have they ever gone off?
- Do you use outlet covers and cabinet locks? If so, what is their purpose?
- Do you have medications with child safety caps? Why are safety caps important?
- Do you keep poisons out of reach or in a safe place? Why?
- Do you keep guns at home? How are they kept safe?

Identify and discuss all the hazards or safety measures you can find.

❑ **Answering the phone**

Answering the phone is a skill that takes practice, and every family has its own rules and ideas about how this should be done. Give your child specific wording to use, and then allow him or her to practice answering the phone while you are present. You might have your child answer in one of the following ways:

- Hello, Holt residence. Who's calling please?
- Hi, this is Lily. Who's calling?
- Hello? Please hold on while I get my parent.

You might use your cell phone to call the home phone from another room, or have a friend or relative call and let your child answer the phone to practice.

❑ **What can you do?**

There are probably lots of ways your child has already learned to be safe. Have your child demonstrate safety skills (or learn ones not yet known), such as the following:

- locking and unlocking the front door
- closing a car door safely
- putting on and taking off a bike helmet
- putting on sunscreen
- buckling a car seat harness or seat belt

Grade 1

Awareness of surroundings

❑ **Use what's available**

This activity uses your imagination to see how ordinary items could be useful in keeping you safe. Take turns with your child finding items in your immediate environment that can be used in an emergency situation. You might point to a chair, for instance, and show how it can be used to help you climb out a window if the door is blocked and you had to escape. You might pick up a broom and a scarf and show how you could tie the scarf onto the broom handle to wave out the window like a flag if you were stranded in a flood. You might find a flashlight for when the power goes out. A blanket can be used to stay warm in a blizzard or to smother a fire on someone's clothes. The goal here is to be creative in finding helpful uses for ordinary items so your child begins to understand the importance of being aware of the surroundings.

❑ **Escape route**

It's a good idea to know alternate ways to exit your home in case of an emergency (such as a fire, intruder, earthquake, flood, etc.). You can make it into a game by setting different parameters and having your child try to devise an escape route. You might say, "How would you get out if the front and back doors were blocked?" or "How would you get out if you were upstairs and you couldn't go downstairs?"

❑ **Follow me**

In this activity, your child gets to develop orienteering skills by finding the way back to a starting point. You might start by walking a few blocks from home and letting your child lead the way back. You can add distance and complexity as your child is ready, and point out various landmarks to navigate by if your child starts to take a wrong turn ("I remember seeing that red house earlier. Do you think we should turn here?") You can also practice navigating while hiking a trail in the woods by letting your child try to retrace your steps back to the trail head. These skills help develop a sense of orientation and awareness of the environment.

Grade 2
Safety when alone or in a group

❑ **Exits and traps**

This energetic activity will help your child begin to recognize how being aware of your surroundings can help you stay safe. Begin in the house and then, if you'd like, you can move the game outdoors. You will be playfully chasing your child as he or she tries to keep from being caught. Encourage your child to look for exits and escape routes, and avoid traps, like dead ends or a blocked passage or stairway. This game should be fun and silly, and you can switch places and let your child chase you. You might let yourself become trapped occasionally to show how that might happen, and what to do if it does (feint right and dart left, put obstacles between you, etc.).

❑ **Lost in a crowd**

Find a photo of a big crowd scene, like a busy mall, a fair, or an amusement park. If you have a place like this near you, you can visit it in person. You and your child will imagine that a child has lost his or her parents. Ask your child what advice you might give to help this lost child find his or her family. You might point to an information or ticket booth, a uniformed employee, a security guard, or another family with children who might be able to help. You can also talk about ways to keep from getting lost: stay together, use the buddy system (stay in pairs), and agree on a meeting place ahead of time in case you are split up.

❑ **Lost in the woods**

If your family lives in a rural area or likes to hike, you can go over the rules about what to do if you get lost in the woods. If possible, practice these skills outside.

- Always carry water and a snack (each person carries his or her own).
- Stop walking and sit with your back against a tree while you wait for someone to find you.
- If you hear your companions nearby or calling your name, yell to help them find you.
- If it gets dark and cold, pile leaves and branches around yourself to keep warm while staying by your tree.

Grade 3

Staying safe in an emergency

- ❏ **Answering the door**

Your family may have specific rules about children answering the door while you are home, and these rules may differ when your child is home alone. As your child gets older, discuss and/or practice what to do when he or she is home alone and someone comes to the door. You may want to have your child write these rules down and post them near the door.

- ❏ **Create a contact list**

Have your child create a contact list of people and phone numbers to call if he or she needs help when home alone. This list may include parent cell phone numbers, relatives, friends, and neighbors. Share your own contact list, which may include emergency services, doctor, veterinarian, etc. Showing what's on your list will help your child see how helpful a contact list can be.

- ❏ **Family emergency plan**

If you haven't already done so, create a family emergency plan together. You will find many helpful resources online and from your community services (police, fire, utility company, etc.). Talk about the best places for the family to gather in case of a hurricane, earthquake, fire, or any other natural disaster common to your area. Have your child create a map that shows where to gather and what to do in each type of emergency.

Notes

Lesson 8 Playground and Community

Your child probably spends a good bit of time out in the community. The activities in this lesson focus on all of the things we can do to keep our communities, and ourselves, safe.

Kindergarten
Playing safe

❑ **Step by step**

Falls are a major source of childhood injuries, but they can often be prevented by helping children learn to pay attention to where they are going. This activity is designed to encourage an awareness of where the body is in relation to obstacles. With your child's help, set up an obstacle course (inside or out) that requires your child to crawl under, climb over, or balance on things. Include as many physical challenges as you can, anything that will require an awareness of the body and the physical environment. The goal is to navigate the course safely.

❑ **Safety rules poster**

Create a poster of safety rules with your child (you can write the rules and your child can illustrate them). Include simply worded rules for toys, sand play, and water. If possible, phrase each rule in the positive (what is allowed) rather than in the negative (what isn't allowed). Some of your family's safety rules might include:

- Share toys and take turns.
- Hand a toy to your friend instead of throwing it.
- Sand stays in the sandbox.
- You can go in the water up to your belly button.
- Put away toys when you are finished with them (so that no one trips on them).

❑ **Map your safe places to play**

Do you have boundaries for your child's play space outdoors? For instance, your child might be allowed to play on the porch, the steps, and the front yard without supervision, and the backyard or barn if you are outside, too. Draw a map with your child, showing the boundaries of the safe play space when playing alone, and have your child color this in. Then add a larger sphere of where your child can play when you are outside but not playing with your child (while you are gardening, hanging laundry, mowing lawn, etc.). Perhaps this line stops at the woods, a creek, or a road. Have your child color this area a different color. Talk about circumstances in which your child will be allowed to go beyond these boundaries. Are there additional rules regarding going into the street or the woods, such as holding hands, wearing shoes, or wearing brightly colored clothing?

Grade 1
Playground safety

❑ **Everyone can play**

It's great fun to visit a playground. Swings, slides, climbing structures, and balancing equipment are excellent for a child's physical development, but playgrounds also present hazards, often from other children using the equipment. Anyone who has walked in front of a swing and gotten knocked over knows this all too well! Take a trip to the playground and while your child is playing, mention the safety rules (you probably do this naturally). When you get home, ask your child to recall as many playground safety rules as possible. These rules might include the following and more:

- Move away after using a slide to make room for the next person coming down.

- Give the swings lots of room when walking past while someone is swinging.
- Leave enough space when following someone up a ladder so you don't accidentally get kicked.
- When running or climbing, be careful not to run into other children (especially those who are smaller) who might be moving slowly and not watching where they are going.

❑ **Egg head**

If your child rides a bike, scooter, horse, skateboard, or skates, wearing a helmet is the best insurance against a head injury. Do this simple experiment to emphasize the importance of protective head gear. Ask your child what would happen if you dropped an egg on the floor. They probably have seen this happen and can readily answer that it will break. Have your child demonstrate this by dropping an egg into a large bowl set on the floor (that way the egg won't be wasted—it can still be used). Next, put an egg into a plastic bag and tape it to the inside of your child's bike helmet. Tape it securely! Have your child gently drop the helmet on the ground so it hits on the top of the helmet. This should be done gently to protect the helmet—the egg will be well protected. Talk about what you observed and why, and how this relates to your child's safety. You might point out that while an egg is much more fragile than a skull (a skull is much harder to break), a brain is a lot more valuable and should be treated very carefully.

❑ **Monkeying around**

Find a place where your child can climb a few feet off the ground and jump off. Make sure it is a height with which your child is comfortable. Perhaps you can use a log or a stump in your backyard, or a climbing structure at the playground. Make sure there is a good landing surface (not concrete or asphalt). First, have your child stand on the ground and imitate a monkey. This will probably entail bent knees, loose swinging arms, and a funny face (you do it, too). Next, tell your child what good climbers monkeys are and how they almost never get hurt jumping down from trees. Explain that you are both going to try to jump like a monkey to help keep your bodies safe. Demonstrate by jumping up onto the stump, bouncing your knees a few times (feel free to add monkey noises), and then jumping down and landing with springy bent knees. Take turns playing monkey and landing with soft, bouncy knees to absorb the shock safely.

Grade 2

Community safety

Crossing the street

Learning to cross the street safely is probably something you have been teaching your child for years. If so, let your child take charge and show you how to cross the street correctly. Make sure he or she follows these steps:

1. Stop at the corner or where there is a crosswalk (or at the side of the road where you are planning to cross). If there is a crosswalk, press the button and wait for the signal.
2. Look to the left for cars. If there are none, look to the right for cars. If there are cars, wait for them to pass and then repeat looking left and right.
3. If there are no cars to the right, look left once more to make sure there are no cars before stepping into the road.
4. Cross the road in a straight line walking briskly so that you are in the lanes of traffic for the least amount of time. Check both ways for oncoming cars as you cross.
5. Step onto the sidewalk or the shoulder of the road before continuing on your way.

If your child doesn't have much experience with crossing the street safely, this is a good time to practice. Take your child through the process step by step, preferably in a place where several streets can be crossed in the course of a short walk.

- [ ] **Who can help? Where to go?**

Ask your child to make a list of all the places he or she normally visits in the course of a week or a month. For each place on the list, have your child write down where to go if help is needed and who to ask. For instance, if your child has been dropped off and is waiting for dance class, where is the best place to go if he or she suddenly feels ill or falls and cuts a knee? Who can be asked for help? Encourage your child to think of multiple options, like this:

Location	Where to go	Who to ask
Dance class	office	receptionist
	dance studio	teacher
	waiting area	another parent

- [ ] **Helping others stay safe**

Even though your child is still fairly young, there are many ways that he or she can help others in the community stay safe. Simple things like holding a small child's hand when crossing the street, or holding a door open for someone with a cane or someone with their hands full, can be helpful. Shoveling an elderly neighbor's walkway after a snowstorm can prevent a fall or injury. Tying a young one's shoe can keep the child from tripping. See how many ways you and your child can come up with, and help your child be on the lookout for ways to keep others in the community safe.

Grade 3
Recognizing dangers

❑ Fast or slow? Stay or go?

This lively activity is all about learning to gauge the risk and make a quick judgment in order to avoid an obstacle. Go outside and make a line with chalk or draw one in the dirt (or create an imaginary line—have your child walk it to clarify where it is). Your child's goal is to walk the length of the line while avoiding a rolling ball. You stand near the middle of the line, off to one side, a few feet away. Roll a large ball, such as a basketball or soccer ball, so it crosses the line just as your child is trying to pass. Start off slowly, rolling the ball in front of your child each time he or she walks the line. (This works best with three people—one to walk the line and two to roll the ball back and forth. If you don't have a second person to roll the ball, you can stand near a fence or wall so the ball bounces back toward you each time.) Your child will have to either speed up or slow down to avoid the moving obstacle (the ball), correctly judging its speed in order to pass safely. When your child starts getting good at avoiding the rolling ball, increase the speed of the ball or send two balls at different times. Be careful not to increase the ball speed too much (or it will hurt if the ball hits your child's legs).

❑ Safe habits

Your third grader probably automatically takes safety precautions without realizing it. This activity brings your child's awareness to these safe habits and reinforces them. Ask your child a series of questions that focus on safe behaviors. Here are a few to get you started, with possible answers your child may give:

- What do you do when you cross the street? (Look both ways.)
- What do you do when we are in a big crowd? (Stay close together.)
- What do you do when your ball rolls into the street? (Don't run after it; check for cars before retrieving it.)
- What do you do if you see a fire? (Go get help; don't try to put it out.)

- What do you do if you spill something on the kitchen floor? (Clean it up before someone slips on it.)
- What do you do when riding in a car? (Buckle the seat belt.)
- What do you do when riding in a boat? (Put on a life vest.)
- What do you do if you break a glass? (Get help to clean it up right away.)

❑ **Danger zone**

Get a large piece of paper and draw a maze of roads on it. You can do this with your child, or your child may want to draw it alone. Next, illustrate as many hazards and obstacles as you can until the scene is filled with dangers, such as:

a crane moving a piano

a load of bricks falling off a truck

a broken bridge

a train jumping the tracks

an open manhole cover

a road closed that leads to a cliff

a stampeding bull

Have fun coming up with a crazy scene—the more implausibly hazardous obstacles, the better. Once it is finished, take turns tracing a safe path through the chaos.

Notes

Lesson 9 Stranger Awareness

The world is filled with lovely, helpful people. However, it is important for your child to learn how to be safe around strangers. This lesson gives you some tools and discussion starters for this important life skill.

Kindergarten

Asking for help

❑ **Help in uniform**

This activity can increase your child's awareness of the many people around us who are likely to be willing and able to help by answering questions and providing assistance. Choose a day when you will be in town or running errands. As you move through your regular activities, keep a running tally of all the people you spot in uniform. This can include police, security guards, maintenance workers, clergy, military personnel, firefighters, EMTs, medical personnel, and store employees. Have your child count how many people in uniform you see.

❑ **How to ask**

Requesting information or assistance from someone you don't know, such as a store clerk or librarian, can be intimidating. Let your child practice making a polite request for assistance or information while you pretend to be a helpful employee. Set up a few different scenarios, like the ones below, and use props if possible.

- Ask for help finding a book in the library.
- Ask how much movie tickets cost.
- Ask a park ranger how to find the trail.

To encourage a realistic scenario, make sure to ask your child questions to clarify what he or she needs ("How many movie tickets do you want to buy? How many adults and how many children will be coming? What time of day will you see the movie?"). Of course, a kindergartener is not likely to be asking for help without an adult supervising, but this fun role-playing game lets your child begin to consider all the times we interact with helpful strangers and how to request assistance.

❑ **Saying no**

Depending on your child's temperament, you may want to have your child practice verbal assertiveness, saying, "No!" loudly to ward off unwanted attention or aggressiveness. (Some children seem to be naturally good at this!) To practice this without unduly concerning your child about stranger danger, you can present imaginary scenarios that he or she will be able to relate to. For instance, you might present the idea of a friend pulling on your arm, a dog on a leash trying to pull you across the road, a bully pushing you aside at the playground, or someone trying to talk you into doing something you don't want to do or that you know is wrong. Instruct your child to hold his or her hands up like a stop sign (which also protects the face), making eye contact, and yelling, "No!" in a strong voice.

Grade 1
Sharing personal information

❑ **What is personal information?**

Before your child can learn to keep personal information private, he or she has to understand what falls under the category of personal information (which covers any details about a particular person). Begin by asking your child to state his or her full name, address, and phone number. (It's okay if your child doesn't know all of these details yet.) Ask your child to say his or her parents' full names, and to name the color and type of car you drive. Explain that this is important personal information and that sometimes adults need this information. For instance, you might provide information like this to doctors, teachers, neighbors, friends, and emergency workers. You can also explain that adults have even more personal information, such as a social security number, medical history, credit card numbers, and bank account information. Discuss how most personal information like this is not given to others unless there is a really good reason.

❑ **Friends and acquaintances**

It can be tricky for a child to distinguish between when it is necessary to provide personal information and when information such as your name and address needs to be kept private. You can phrase this as a choice question to help make the distinctions more pronounced: "Would you give your name to a police officer if you were lost? Would you give it to a person driving by who stopped his or her car and asked your name?" Talk about why the answer to one scenario is a "yes" and to the other is a "no." Keep explanations simple, if possible: "Yes, it is okay to give a police officer your name if you are lost because that will help the officer find your home. No, it is not okay to give your name to someone driving by because then they might pretend to be your friend and try to get you to drive away with them." Use your own good judgment about how to give your child enough information to be safe without unnecessarily frightening or confusing your child.

❑ **From stranger to friend**

There are lots of times when strangers become friends—in fact, just about every friend was once a stranger! Ask your child to list one good friend (or several). Talk about what makes this person a good friend. You might mention shared experiences, going over to each other's houses, meeting family and friends, doing something kind for one another, etc. Next, ask your child to list one or two acquaintances (people you know but not very well) and point out at least one stranger. Talk about these different distinctions: friend, acquaintance, stranger. Discuss the different kinds of information you share with a friend, an acquaintance, and a stranger, and the different types of help you might request from each. If appropriate to your family situation, you might want to also discuss people with whom you interact online, and what the rules and boundaries are for these online acquaintances.

Grade 2
Who can you trust?

❑ You never know

Have you ever played the game where you make up imaginary stories about strangers you see on a bus or in the airport? This game helps underscore, in a playful way, the axiom, "Don't judge a book by its cover." Take turns with your child making up stories about people you see. Make sure that some of your stories go against stereotype and include some dangerous imaginary escapades. For instance, you might imagine that the pierced, tattooed young woman at the coffee shop is a famous author of children's books, or the old man walking his dog in the park is on his way to rob a bank and the dog will run away with the money in a little backpack. Keep it light, silly, and fun. The message will sink in without your coming right out and saying, "Don't judge people based on their looks."

❑ Making choices

Using photos of busy places or a book with well-populated illustrations (such as the *Where's Waldo?* books), point out to your child the people whom you would choose to ask for help. Explain your thinking process as you make your choices, which will probably be based on behavior rather than looks. For instance, you might choose an adult with a child over a solitary adult because you think the parent might be more prepared to help you and your child. You might choose an older person over a younger one (or vice versa) because you think that person would be more experienced or able to help. You probably wouldn't ask for help from someone who looked upset or angry, or someone who was in a hurry or was busy talking on the phone. There are no right or wrong answers in this activity since every situation and every person is different. While the previous activity focused on prejudice and emphasized the importance of not making assumptions based on looks, the goal here is to expose your child to the reasoning process that you use when figuring out whom to approach.

❑ **When adults need help**

This activity gives you a chance to discuss scenarios where an adult might ask for help. In general, unknown adults should not ask children for help when the children's parents are not present, and you may want to enforce this idea by advising your child to always find an adult when someone needs help. If you'd like, you can present this by giving examples of adults asking children for help or offering something in order to lure them into a car ("Can you help me look for my puppy?" "I have all of these cookies. Do you want some?"), and providing your child with a stock response (running away or responding with a firm, "No!"). Alternately, you may want to keep this on a more positive note by giving examples of when and how children can help adults if their parents are close by, such as picking up something that was dropped, retrieving something that has fallen into a small space, or carrying something heavy.

Grade 3
Recognizing risky situations

❑ **Warning signs**

Learning to recognize a risky situation will help your child be able to avoid one. Come up with a list of warning signs, and ask for your child's input as well—you might be surprised to find that your child is more aware than you expect. Here are some warning signs of a risky situation:

- dark empty street
- dead-end alley
- walking alone at night
- going far away from where the adults are
- going far from home or not knowing how to return home

❑ **Getting to a safe place**

Using the list of warning signs in the previous activity, or ones you generate, ask your child how a person in this situation could get home safely (or come up with a plan together). Of course, it is highly unlikely your third grader would end up in situations like these, but discussing it now gives your child knowledge and empowerment to act safely in the future.

❑ **Speaking up**

This is a role-playing game where you pretend to be someone who is trying to talk your child into doing something wrong or unsafe. Start with a fairly innocuous circumstance (trying to convince your child to take an extra cookie without permission, for example) and work your way up to situations with more dire consequences: going somewhere without telling a parent, stealing something, smoking a cigarette. Use your discretion in coming up with realistic scenarios and in figuring out the amount of pressure to put on your child with these scenarios. Switch places, if necessary, to model for your child clear, assertive language to use in resisting pressure. Some children feel that if they refuse to do something, they need to provide an explanation, so a helpful phrase to teach your child is, "I'm just not comfortable doing that." This can work well in a wide variety of situations.

Lesson 10 Healthy Home

As a parent, you work hard to create a home that is healthy and happy. Your child can help, too! Here are some activities to bring your child's awareness to what it takes to create a healthy living environment.

Kindergarten

Cooperation and house rules

❑ **You make the rules**

Every house has rules, although they often aren't written down. Create a poster with some of your house rules, such as taking off your shoes when coming inside, putting your dirty dishes in the dishwasher, or not watching TV until after dinner. Have your child illustrate it. Talk about how house rules help keep things running smoothly. You might ask your child to come up with a new house rule.

❑ **You rock**

One way to encourage cooperation at home is to celebrate small acts of helpfulness or good deeds. Collect a large pile of small stones (nuts or shells are also good). Put them in a bowl next to a large, empty glass jar, like a quart Mason jar. Every time someone does something thoughtful or helpful, a rock gets placed in the glass jar. When the glass jar is filled to the brim, do something fun to celebrate: a hike, a pizza, a family game night, etc. Empty the jar and start over.

❑ **Family roles**

Everyone likes to be appreciated for what they do to help out around the house. This activity focuses on the contributions each member of the family makes to create a harmonious and orderly household. Ask your child to draw a picture of each family member and to list the ways in which each person helps out around the house (you can write things down under each person's picture). Your child might want to take on new chores to add to his or her list, such as feeding a pet, collecting the mail, or sweeping the front steps.

Grade 1
Contributing to a healthy home

❑ **Basic cleaning**

Children are often interested in helping with chores. You can teach your child basic cleaning skills. You'll find some listed below and you can come up with ones that suit your family. Show your child how to do the chore step by step, including assembling the supplies and putting them away afterwards.

- wiping the table and counter
- sweeping the floor
- washing dishes
- vacuuming the rug
- dusting shelves

❑ **Laundry list**

While your child might be too small to take care of the laundry, there are lots of ways he or she can help. Involving your child in laundry chores can lead to conversations about how to minimize dirty laundry and conserve energy. Here are some of the ways your child can get involved:

- collect dirty towels from the bathroom
- sort dirty laundry into washing piles
- measure and pour laundry detergent
- help fold sheets and towels
- match clean socks
- put clean clothes away

❑ Helpful habits

There are many things a person can do—even a little person—to help a house stay clean and tidy. Brainstorm with your child a list of helpful habits. Write them down in a decorated list to serve as a reminder to everyone. Here are some examples:

- Wipe feet (or take off shoes) when coming indoors.
- Pick up things you drop.
- Wipe up things you spill.
- Put things back where you found them.
- Put your clothes where they belong when you take them off.

Grade 2

Keeping a clean room

❑ Who cares?

To emphasize the pleasure and practicality of a neat, clean room, have your child help you make up a funny story about a wildly untidy room. Here are some opening lines to get you started, or come up with your own.

- Once there was a boy who declared he'd never clean his room again, and to his great surprise, his parents agreed. The first day, he left his dirty clothes on the floor, and the second day, he...
- Once there was a woman who decided to have an immense party with all sorts of decorations and games and food (elaborate on this). When the party was over, there was a humongous mess left behind. The woman simply did not have the energy to clean up, so she just went to bed. The next day...
- There once was a girl who loved animals so much that every animal she found, she brought into her room to live...

You might want to end your story with a lesson ("...and the room was so messy, they never saw the boy again") or with things being put to rights: "Eventually he'd had enough! He couldn't find anything anymore, not even his favorite marble. So he started cleaning, and he cleaned and he cleaned and he cleaned until finally everything was back where it belonged. And he finally found his favorite marble, under the bed."

❑ **Bed clothes and window washing**

Making a bed can vary from hotel-like efficiency to tossing a comforter more or less in the middle of the bed. Whatever your family's style, your child can be taught to remove sheets and pillowcases for washing, and help put them back on the bed when clean. The reward for this physically demanding job is the sweet smell and tidy, smooth feel of clean bed linens.

Another job that children can be taught is window washing. (If you are worried about your child having contact with cleaning chemicals, you can get a nontoxic cleaner or use vinegar and water.) Window washing is a very energetic task, but washing windows with you on one side of the glass (inside or outside) and your child on the other makes it more fun.

❑ **Bin there**

Do your child's toys, clothes, or art supplies continually spill out of their assigned spot (or rarely get put away)? Creating an organization system with labeled bins or baskets can help you regain order and encourage your child to maintain it. Begin by choosing one area to reorganize. Have your child sort things in a way that seems logical, and then provide bins or baskets for each pile. Your child can create colorful labels for each.

Grade 3
Clean habits

❑ **Make your life easier**

Help your child identify two to three areas in the home that are hard to keep clean. Ask your child to think about what really bothers him or her about these areas. Perhaps your child's wastepaper basket keeps overflowing, or jewelry keeps getting tangled, or sports equipment is in such a jumble that it is hard to find anything. Choose one thing to fix and brainstorm a solution, plus come up with a list of new behaviors (habits) that will help keep things organized. For instance, for the problem of the overflowing wastepaper, you might decide a larger basket will be a good solution, and new habits that help to reduce waste could be using both sides of the paper, and emptying the basket into the recycling bin at the end of each day or week.

- [ ] **Habit forming**

Sometimes we want to form a new habit but it's hard to know how to begin. Help your child identify something that he or she would like to begin doing regularly. Choose something simple, like getting into the habit of hanging up a jacket or putting away shoes when coming inside, brushing the dog each day, or putting books back on the shelf after reading time. Next, brainstorm ways to support the forming of this habit, which may include some or all of the following:

- Put up a reminder note where it will easily be seen.
- Connect the new habit to one that is already formed. For instance, your child probably closes the door every time he or she comes inside. Add onto this close-the-door habit by putting a shoe rack there so that closing the door and taking off shoes will become a two-step process. If it is already a habit to give the dog a treat after coming in from a walk, then put the dog brush next to the treats.
- Create a system that rewards the behavior when it is completed, such as favorite fuzzy slippers that are kept where the shoes belong—when the shoes are put away, the fuzzy slippers can be put on. Or perhaps after the dog is brushed, your child can give the dog a treat, which is as fun for the child as it is for the dog!
- Put into place a speed bump of sorts so that if the behavior hasn't been done, the next (desired) thing can't happen. For instance, snack can't be served until the shoes are changed, and the dog can't be allowed into the living room until it has been brushed.
- Congratulate each success. Do a happy dance, pat yourself on the back, or give a little chant or song, like "I did it! I did it!"
- Keep practicing until the habit becomes automatic.

Check back in a week to see how well this habit is being integrated into daily life, and find new ways to support it, if necessary.

❏ **Make it your own**

In this activity, your child will create a room decoration for his or her bedroom. Taking the time to make the room a more welcoming place can help your child want to keep it neat. Ask your child for ideas on what to do or create to make the room look nicer, or suggest one of these:

- put up artwork on the walls
- pick flowers and put them in a vase on the dresser or windowsill
- hang a crystal in the window
- draw a name sign for the door

Lesson

People Who Help

The health, safety, and well-being of individuals and communities is dependent, to a large extent, on the people who serve the community. This lesson looks at the good work performed by police officers, firefighters, paramedics, and health care providers in your community.

Kindergarten

Police officers

❑ **Hello and thank you**

The goal of this activity is to help your child appreciate the important work of police officers and to feel comfortable around them. If you know a police officer or live in a place where you often see officers on patrol, have your child greet the officer and introduce him- or herself. You might prepare ahead of time by talking about the good work police do to serve the community and keep it safe. You might also come up with a few questions you or your child might ask, such as the following

- How long have you been a police officer?
- How long did you study and train for the job?
- What do you like best about your job?

Afterward, encourage your child to draw a card of thanks and appreciation, and bring it to the local police department.

❑ **Doing their jobs**

While much of what police officers do is difficult and dangerous, there are many stories of officers helping people in heart-warming ways: reuniting a lost child and parents, staying with someone who is injured and scared until help arrives; rescuing a cat from a tree; helping local communities through youth charities, etc. Do some research online for stories of police heroism or get a book out of the library, and share with your child some of the many facets of police work.

❑ **How can I help?**

Police officers rely on citizen support and cooperation in many ways. Talk to your child about the ways that ordinary people can make the challenging job of a police officer a little easier. Here are some ways that adults and children can help, and you might think of others:

- Know and obey the laws.
- Know your neighbors and keep watch on your neighborhood.
- Call the police if there is trouble or someone needs help.
- Help an investigation by carefully describing what happened.
- Keep guns in the home locked up and away from children.
- Be friendly and respectful to officers.
- If there is an emergency, remember the police are there to help you (don't hide from them).

Grade 1
Firefighters

❑ **Hello and thank you**

As with the similarly titled exercise above, the goal of this activity is to help your child appreciate the important work of firefighters. If possible, arrange for your child to meet a firefighter and talk about the job, the training, the uniform and safety gear, and the equipment. Ask your child to draw a card of appreciation, and bring it to the local fire department.

❑ **Doing their jobs**

Arrange to visit the fire station for a tour to find out more about what firefighters do. As with police work, much of what firefighters do is difficult and dangerous, but there are many stories of firefighters helping people save their homes, their pets, and their belongings as well as their lives. Find a book in the library on firefighters and the exceptional work they do for their communities.

❑ **How can I help?**

Talk to your child about things you can do to prevent fires or to make the job of a firefighter a little easier. Here are some ideas:

- Don't play with matches or lighters.
- Learn about fire safety.
- Call the fire department if you see a fire.
- If there is a fire in your house, leave immediately and call 911 from another house or a cell phone (a 911 operator will alert the fire department).
- Don't go back into a burning building to rescue a pet or retrieve belongings.
- Keep a smoke detector in the house and change the batteries twice a year.
- Don't leave candles unattended.
- In an emergency, remember the firefighters are there to help you (don't hide from them).

Grade 2
Paramedics

❑ **First responders in action**

In this action-packed activity, your child gets to pretend to be an EMT (emergency medical technician) or a paramedic (highly trained medical professionals who have over 1,000 hours additional training beyond the EMT certification). You get to be the victim, putting yourself in all sorts of imaginary difficulties: trapped in a car that has flipped on its side, suffering a broken ankle while hiking, having a broken arm from falling down the stairs, or whatever other dire straights you and your child can think of. First, give your child a basic rundown of rescue protocol:

1. Check for breathing and control bleeding.
2. Check for injuries and immobilize them.

3. Transport injured person to the ambulance.
4. Accompany injured person to the hospital and report to the ER doctors.

Next, gather up a few supplies to add some realism (pretend phones so you can call for help, bandages and splints, a "stretcher" of couch cushions or a board, etc.). This activity is not intended to give your child much factual information about emergency medical services but to allow him or her the experience of helping in a simulated emergency situation.

❑ **Canine search and rescue**

Dogs have been used for search and rescue efforts for hundreds of years. Find a book or search online for information and stories about dogs that are part of search and rescue teams. Talk about what dogs can do to assists humans and ways in which canines are particularly well-suited to this work.

❑ **What to expect in the ER**

Visits to the hospital emergency room are sometimes part of a lively, active childhood. While you may not want to visit an ER on a field trip (it's impossible to know what kind of traumas may be present at any given time), you can give your child a sense of what to expect in the ER, and of the many reasons you might find yourself there. For example, people visit the ER to treat an allergic reaction; a cut requiring stiches at night, during a holiday, or on the weekend when the doctor's office is closed; an accident requiring immediate medical attention; a sudden serious illness, etc. Talk your child through the steps of triage (determining the urgency of each individual's injury), intake (giving information on family, insurance, health issues, etc.), exam, and treatment. Find a library book with photos to help you explain the many machines, people, sounds, smells, and procedures that might be part of an ER visit.

Grade 3

Health care providers

❑ Who's who at the hospital

The hospital can seem a confusing, hectic place, but spending some time in a hospital lobby can help you begin to notice and appreciate the organization of the vast number of health care providers involved in the smooth operation of a hospital. Take your child to a hospital lobby and find a comfortable spot to sit and watch the comings and goings. Point out the different people who work there, and, if you can, describe some of what they do. Discuss the purposes of the various wings or departments of the hospital. Express an appreciation for all those who work hard each day to help people be well.

❑ Protecting themselves

Medical professionals have to protect their own health while working to help others be well. Explain to your child that the health care providers have many, many rules to follow to help them stay healthy, such as disinfecting surfaces between patients, washing hands frequently, sterilizing equipment, disposing of needles safely, etc. Talk about the protective gear used by medical professionals: gloves, masks, and goggles. If possible, get a pair of latex gloves, goggles (safety glasses), and a surgical mask (use the type of mask sold in hardware stores to protect from chemical fumes or make a simple cloth mask with ribbon ties) for your child to use during dramatic play.

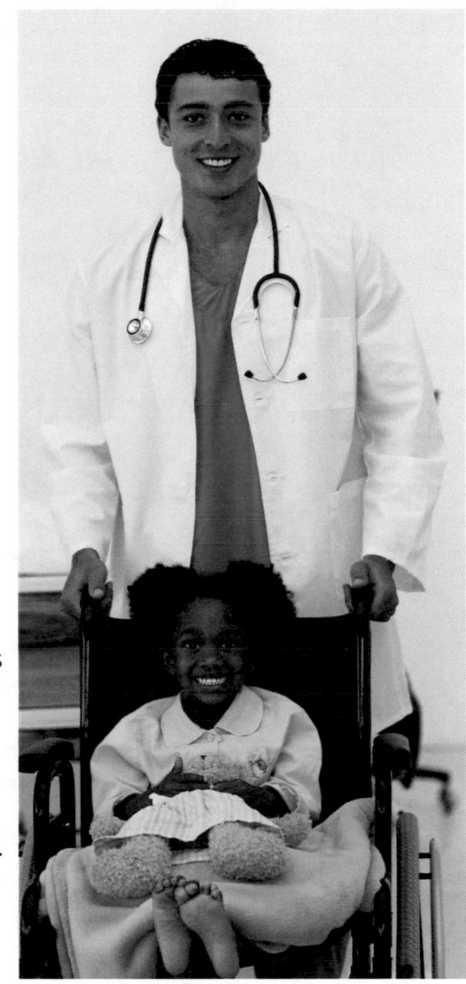

❑ Sad or glad: reasons for being in the hospital

There are many reasons to visit a hospital, and while often people are there because they are in pain or something is wrong, that is not always the case. Ask your child to list reasons for being in the hospital, and divide them into the following categories. Add your own ideas until each category has two to three entries.

- Sad: car accident; fire injuries, heart attack; cancer treatments.
- Glad: having a baby (or visiting a new baby); getting a preventive health screening; having surgery to fix a problem; visiting a patient.

Notes

Lesson 12 Unit II Review: Personal Safety

Check off the activities you completed in the second unit (lessons 7–11). Take some time to explore more fully any topics in which your child was particularly interested, or revisit favorite activities. You may want to try a new activity around the topic of personal safety.

Lesson 7: Personal Awareness

KINDERGARTEN	**Home safety** ❑ A safe home ❑ Answering the phone ❑ What can you do?
GRADE 1	**Awareness of surroundings** ❑ Use what's available ❑ Escape route ❑ Follow me
GRADE 2	**Safety when alone or in a group** ❑ Exits and traps ❑ Lost in a crowd ❑ Lost in the woods
GRADE 3	**Staying safe in an emergency** ❑ Answering the door ❑ Create a contact list ❑ Family emergency plan

Lesson 8: Playground and Community

KINDERGARTEN	**Playing safe** ❑ Step by step ❑ Safety rules poster ❑ Map your safe places to play
GRADE 1	**Playground safety** ❑ Everyone can play ❑ Egg head ❑ Monkeying around
GRADE 2	**Community safety** ❑ Crossing the street ❑ Who can help? Where to go? ❑ Helping others stay safe
GRADE 3	**Recognizing dangers** ❑ Fast or slow? Stay or go? ❑ Safe habits ❑ Danger zone

Lesson 9: Stranger Awareness

KINDERGARTEN	**Asking for help** ❏ Help in uniform ❏ How to ask ❏ Saying no
GRADE 1	**Sharing personal information** ❏ What is personal information? ❏ Friends and acquaintances ❏ From stranger to friend
GRADE 2	**Who can you trust?** ❏ You never know ❏ Making choices ❏ When adults need help
GRADE 3	**Recognizing risky situations** ❏ Warning signs ❏ Getting to a safe place ❏ Speaking up

Lesson 10: Healthy Home

KINDERGARTEN	**Cooperation and house rules** ❑ You make the rules ❑ You rock ❑ Family roles
GRADE 1	**Contributing to a healthy home** ❑ Basic cleaning ❑ Laundry list ❑ Helpful habits
GRADE 2	**Keeping a clean room** ❑ Who cares? ❑ Bed clothes and window washing ❑ Bin there
GRADE 3	**Clean habits** ❑ Make your life easier ❑ Habit forming ❑ Make it your own

Lesson 11: People Who Help

KINDERGARTEN	**Police officers** ❏ Hello and thank you ❏ Doing their jobs ❏ How can I help?
GRADE 1	**Firefighters** ❏ Hello and thank you ❏ Doing their jobs ❏ How can I help?
GRADE 2	**Paramedics** ❏ First responders in action ❏ Canine search and rescue ❏ What to expect in the ER
GRADE 3	**Health care providers** ❏ Who's who at the hospital ❏ Protecting themselves ❏ Sad or glad: reasons for being in the hospital

Notes

Lesson 13 Nutrition

For the next few lessons, you'll be exploring healthy food choices, beginning with a look at nutrition and what the body needs to maintain good health.

Kindergarten

Healthy food, clean water, fresh air

❑ **Fresh food**

Have your child draw a picture of all the raw foods he or she likes to eat. Raw foods are foods that are eaten fresh, without cooking or processing. Many fruits and vegetables fall into this category. Next, have your child go on a search to find all the fresh foods in your home and garden (this includes plants that may not be blooming currently, such as fruit trees or berry plants), and then draw a picture of them, circling the foods that are favorites.

❑ **Water, water everywhere**

Collect water in glass jars from as many nearby sources as you can: tap, rainwater, outside spigot or hose, river, ocean, pond, puddle, etc. Label each jar with the water source. Place them side by side on a window sill or table and carefully examine each, looking for differences in color and sediment. Talk about which ones are safe to drink and why some water is safe and some is not. Explain what could happen to your body if you drink unclean or unfiltered water.

❑ **Smell test**

Find several places where the air will smell different and visit them over the course of the next week. You might visit your yard, a meadow in the sun, the forest, a bog or swamp, an outdoor fire, a busy street, a city, etc. In each location, take a few deep breaths and draw your child's attention to how the air smells. Talk about how air quality is affected by cars, factories, and other effects of humanity. Speak simply about the need for fresh, healthy air and how trees and plants help filter and cleanse the air. There is no need to go into greater detail—this is mainly an exercise in sensory awareness.

Grade 1
Balanced diet

❑ **I need/I want**

Ask your child, "What food do you love to eat? If you could eat anything, what would you want?" Write down the answers. Next, ask, "What food does your body need?" Make a second list, gently guiding your child toward accurate answers, such as fruits, vegetables, water, grains, and meat, eggs, milk, or cheese (depending on your family's diet). Have your child draw or cut out pictures to show each of the items on these two lists, and make a collage with wants on one side and needs on the other. Foods that are on both lists can go in the middle. This is a great opportunity to talk about making good food choices.

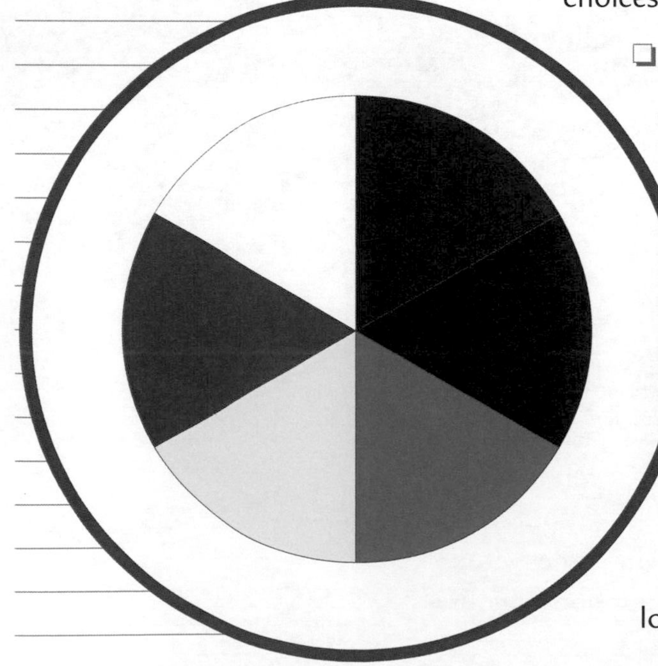

❑ **Keeping track**

Help your child create a food log. Make it colorful and easy to use. Have your child write down everything eaten in a single day (or over several days). You can also include a tally of drinks. Talk about what the food log reveals. Is there a good balance of foods from the different food groups?

❑ **The color plate**

Have your child draw a large circle on a white piece of paper, and divide it into six sections (with equal wedges like a pie, or in any way you like). Lightly color the sections as follows: red, purple/blue, green, yellow, and orange. The final section will remain white. Begin brainstorming together to name fruits and vegetables that match these colors, and write or draw them in each section. For instance, strawberries would go in the red section, eggplant would go in the purple/blue section, coconut in the white, etc. Throughout the next few meals, have your child count how many different colored foods are on his or her plate.

Grade 2

Six essential nutrients

- [ ] **What are the six essential nutrients?**

Share this information with your child. Help him or her come up with food examples from each meal to list under each category.

- **Carbohydrates** (or carbs) are the main source of energy for the body, feeding muscles, nerves, and the brain. Main sources are grains (bread, rice, pasta, etc.) and starchy vegetables, like potatoes, corn, or squash. Carbohydrates are converted to sugars in the body for quick energy, or stored as fat if not needed right away.
- **Protein** is important for healthy cells and for building and repairing muscles and body tissues. Proteins are made up of amino acids. Sources of protein include meat, fish, dairy, beans (including soy products), and eggs.
- **Fats** are stored energy, and essential for the absorption of certain vitamins, such a A, D, and E. Healthy sources of fat are nuts, seeds, fish, avocados, and olives.
- **Vitamins** are found in a wide array of fruits and vegetables, and play a vital role in the body's health by providing nourishment for overall growth and health and for regulating body processes.
- **Minerals** are important for building bones, teeth, and blood. Like vitamins, rich sources of minerals are found in a wide variety of fruits and vegetables.
- **Water** is needed on a daily basis. It is essential for transporting nutrients to cells and for removing waste products from the body. Water makes up more than half of your body weight. In addition to drinking water, sources of water are found in

many fruits (think about how juicy a watermelon is!) as well as soups, tea, and juices.

- ❑ **Favorites list**

  Make a chart with sections for each of the six essential nutrients. Have your child list as many favorite foods as possible. Write each one down on a slip of paper, and then glue each strip into the nutrient category where it best fits. There will be overlap, of course, but this activity will help your child begin to understand food categories and sources of the six essential nutrients.

- ❑ **Food group hopscotch**

  Using chalk, draw a grid of connected squares on the sidewalk, two squares wide and three long. Make them large enough to fit your child's feet but not too much bigger. Label them as follows:

  Have your child stand outside the grid (where it says *start*) and name a food. As you call out the food groups to which it belongs, your child has to jump one foot on each of those squares or two feet on

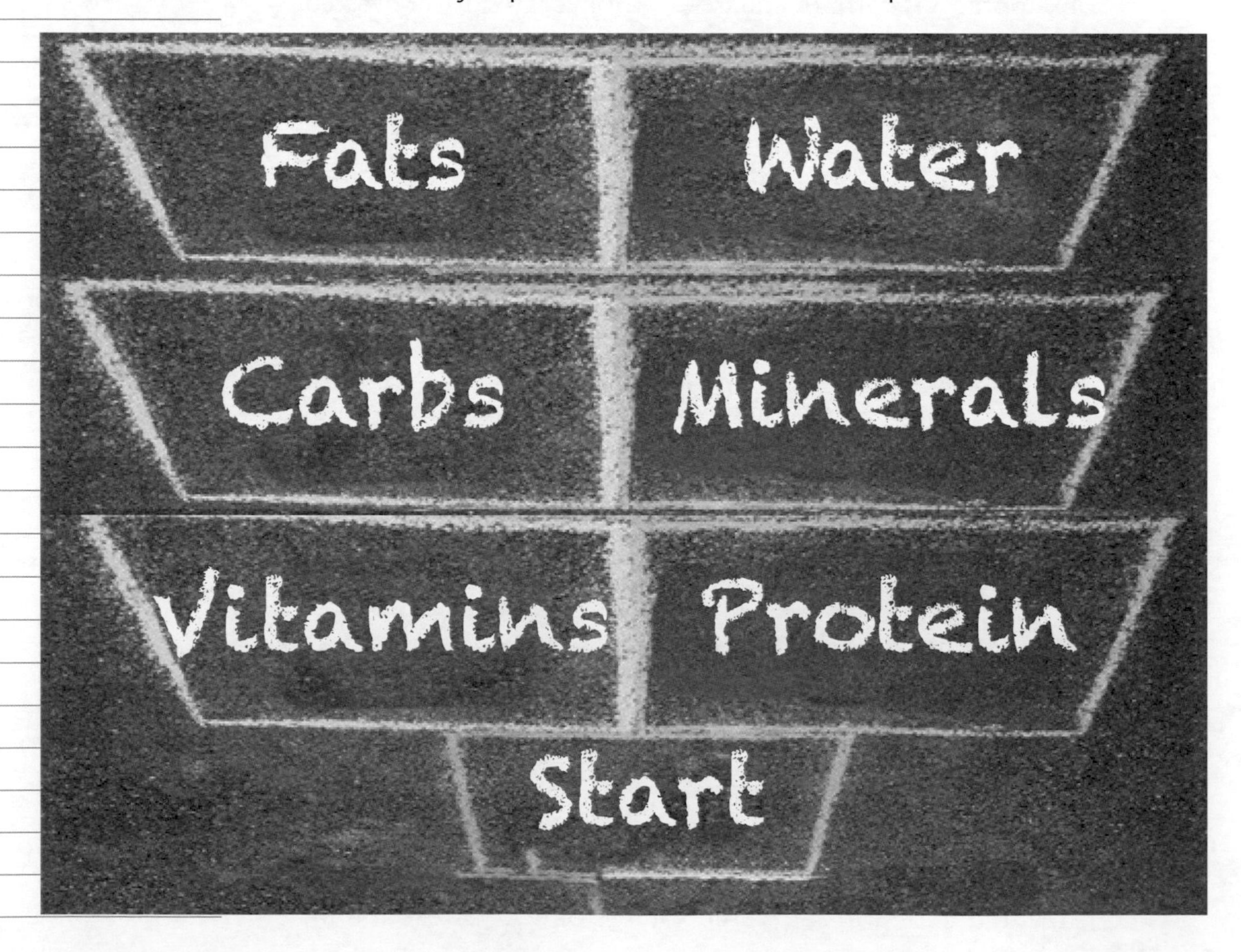

two squares, but only those squares. For instance, if your child says, "Apple," you would say, "Vitamins and minerals," and your child has to hop on those two squares (one after the other, or both at the same time). Once you two get the hang of the game, see if you can switch, with you calling out a food and your child guessing which squares to use.

Grade 3

Weight management

❑ **Calories in/calories out**

Eating and drinking give our bodies the daily calories we need to have the energy to function. But if all we did was eat, the calorie intake would soon result in unhealthy weight gain (not to be confused with necessary and normal weight gain experienced by all healthy, growing children). Give your child the picture of a balance scale with food on one side and ask your child what might go on the other side to balance the calorie intake and consume the extra calories (the ones not needed for regular growth). Have your child list (verbally or on paper) all the ways he or she expends calories in the form of energy. Get your child started with mentioning simple things like walking, biking, and stretching. Your child's list might include things like running, climbing, dancing, gymnastics, swimming, or playing with the dog. Talk about which activities use the most energy/calories and which use the least.

❑ **Good fats, bad fats**

This research activity lets you explore the essential role of fats. Search online or help your child find information in the library about fat sources, both plant and animal. See if you can find out how plant and animal fats differ (without getting into too much of the complex science behind it). Talk about customary sources of fat in your family's diet.

❑ **All filled up**

Have you ever heard someone push back from the table and say, "I'm stuffed"? Have you ever eaten to the point of feeling uncomfortable? Many people have had the experience of eating past the point of feeling full. Over the next few meals, try each of these experiments with your child (one per meal):

- Eat a smaller portion than usual and wait ten minutes before eating more.
- Eat more slowly, chewing more fully, and putting your fork down in between bites.
- Drink a glass of water directly before a meal.

After each experiment, talk about how these different ways of approaching a meal affect the way you feel. Do you feel more satisfied with less food? Are you still hungry? Did one experiment work better for you than the others? Use these questions to launch a conversation about learning to sense when you've eaten enough to be satisfied, no more, no less.

Lesson 14 Food Choices

The following activities focus on evaluating food choices and encouraging children to become more aware of the healthy options available to them.

Kindergarten
Food groups

❑ Food group faces

Using rice cakes or a slice of bread, show your child how to build a snack that uses all the food groups. Creating a face shape is a fun way to do this. Here are a few possibilities—mix and match for lots of different faces:

- Head (carbs): rice cake, bread, tortilla
- Face (protein): cream cheese, peanut butter, almond butter, hummus
- Eyes (fats): olives, almonds, sunflower seeds
- Nose and mouth (vitamins and minerals): raisins, apple slice, cucumber, red pepper

Encourage your child to experiment with different foods and faces, and then enjoy the healthy snack.

❑ Building a meal

Create your own mix-and-match meal cards. Have your child choose three pieces of colored paper (three different colors). Your child can fold each paper in half, and then in half again, and then open it up and cut along the folded lines to create four "cards." Choose one color for fruits and veggies (vitamins and minerals), one color for meat, dairy, and plant-based protein, and one color for grains (carbohydrates). Have your child draw or find a photo of four different foods he or she likes for each category. Once all twelve cards are completed, take turns drawing three cards (one of each color) and building an imaginary meal from the three ingredients. If possible, let your child help prepare a meal based on the cards.

❑ **What do animals eat?**

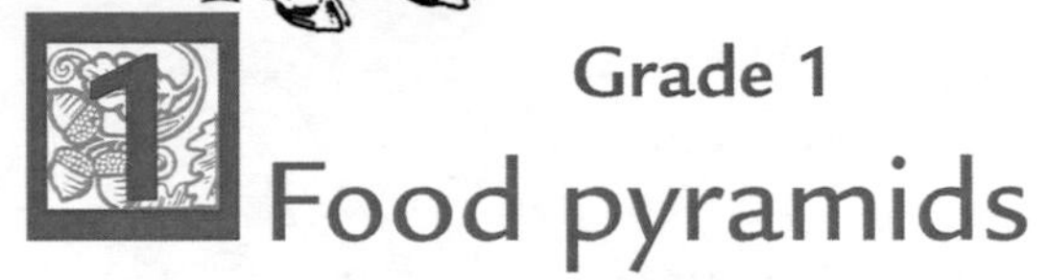

Explore the question of what animals need to eat to be healthy and strong. Does a cow or a sheep need to eat from all the food groups like we do? Visit a farm to talk to the farmer and see what the animals eat. How is it similar to human food? How is it different?

Grade 1
Food pyramids

❑ **Draw food pyramids**

The food pyramid that most parents today grew up with has been turned on its head, literally. Search online and print out a few different food pyramids, including the traditional pyramid, the Mediterranean pyramid, the inverted pyramid, and the pyramid alternative, the food plate. Have your child draw the pyramid or plate design that best fits your family's diet. (An excellent online resource for food pyramids is Oldways Preservation Trust; see the recommended reading list at the end of this book for more details.)

❑ **Sweet is a treat**

Many people of all ages enjoy eating sweets. To help your child understand the role of sugars in your diet and the need for moderation, begin by taking out all the different types of sugar you use in your household and line them up. You may have white sugar, brown sugar, honey, maple syrup, molasses, stevia, agave, or other sweeteners. Let your child take a tiny taste of each one and talk about the differences in appearance, how each is processed, and the effect each has on the body (if you know it). Next, take out all the processed or prepared foods in the house that have sugar or corn syrup listed in the ingredients. This may include cereals, dressings, soups, bread, yogurt, and crackers. This pile may be surprisingly large!

Talk about the prevalence of sugar in the modern diet, and let your child know that unlike the six essential nutrients, the body doesn't need sugar to be healthy. In fact, too much sugar can be harmful to the body. While your child helps you put everything away, brainstorm ways to moderate sugar consumption. You might discuss serving smaller dessert portions, eating dessert only on certain days of the week, reducing sugar in non-dessert foods, and using honey or natural sweeteners like maple syrup in recipes in place of white or brown sugar. This is also an excellent time to talk about natural food-based sugars—mainly found in fruits, especially dried fruits, which can taste very sweet—and why they are a good alternative to treats with added sugar.

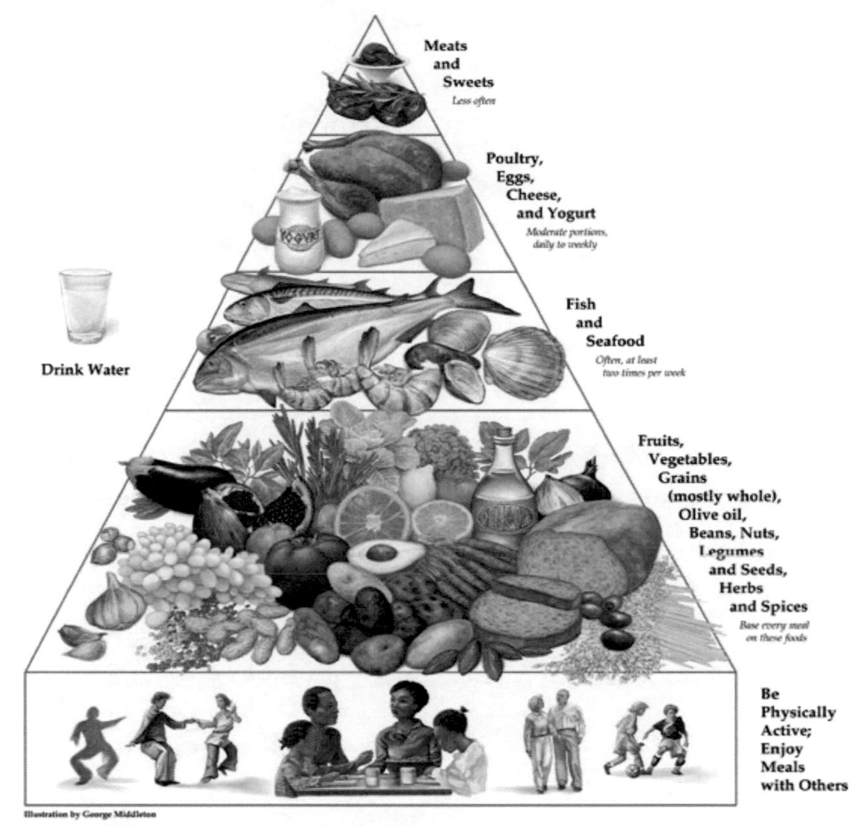

❑ **Salty or sweet?**

This is a game in which you take turns presenting two different food choices—one salty, one sweet—and choosing which you'd rather eat. For instance, you might ask your child, "Would you rather have a pretzel or a cookie?" Your child gets to choose one or the other, and then ask you something different, like, "Would you rather eat nachos or ice cream?" Continue for a few rounds and see if either of you shows a pattern of preferring salty or sweet foods. The goal is a greater awareness of taste preferences that are likely to influence food choices.

Grade 2

Building your food pyramid

❑ **What did I eat today?**

Have your child draw a food pyramid or plate (see the first activity under grade 1 above), dividing it into sections and labeling each section. Throughout the day after each meal, your child can write down the foods he or she eats in the appropriate section of the pyramid or plate. At the end of the day, review the balance of the daily food choices.

❑ **Draw your personal pyramid**

Make a list of food choices for one day. Divide the foods on the list into the following categories: grains, vegetables and fruit, protein (meat, fish, eggs, dairy, and plant-based protein), fats, and sugars. Count up the number of food items in each category (How many times were grains eaten? How many times was protein consumed?). Draw a simple pyramid and divide it into five sections. In the largest section, write the name of the food category that had the most servings eaten, and list the foods eaten. For the next largest section, label the food category with the next highest number of items, and record them. Continue up to the top of the pyramid and the food category with the fewest servings eaten. Use this personal pyramid to start a conversation about how the daily food intake fits into the desired balanced diet.

❑ **So many ways to eat healthy**

Many families choose alternative diets, such as vegetarian, vegan, gluten-free, or pescetarian (a mainly vegetarian diet that includes fish). You may want to experiment by following one or more of these alternative diets for one day or one week. Discuss the health benefits of each and how it feels to eat according to a specific diet. Another option is to choose one diet and learn more about it.

Grade 3

Meal planning

❑ Choosing ingredients

Let your child choose a cookbook, either from your own collection or from the library, and find a recipe that sounds tasty and is not too difficult to make (you'll be helping). Have your child copy the list of ingredients and discuss options for ingredient sources. For instance, if the recipe calls for spinach, would you use fresh spinach from the garden or market, packaged spinach from the store, or frozen spinach? Would you buy organic spinach, or perhaps spinach from the farmer's market that isn't organic but is locally grown without pesticides? Consider the possible sources for each ingredient (herbs: fresh? dried? homegrown? powdered?) and then discuss how you make the decision when choosing ingredients.

If possible, procure the ingredients and prepare the recipe together. If it is a simple recipe, you might do an experiment and cook one batch with fresh organic ingredients and one with packaged, processed ingredients, and see if you notice a difference.

❑ Timing it right

Let your child help you plan dinner one night. Once the menu is set, ask your child to guess what gets prepared first. Discuss the complexities of getting a simple meal on the table with various dishes ready to serve all at the same time. Let your child take charge of one dish, if possible, and work together to coordinate the use of the cutting board, stove, or oven.

❑ **Something for everyone**

Give your child a clipboard and have him or her poll all the family members (including self!) about which foods they prefer and which ones they dislike or need to avoid (food allergies, for instance). Have your child devise a dinner menu that works for everyone. If you want to present a greater challenge, have your child poll a larger group of extended family and friends, and create the menu for an imaginary party where there is something to eat for everyone.

Lesson 15 Enjoying Food

Learning to prepare food is a valuable skill, and even young children can contribute. Remind children to wash their hands before handling food.

Kindergarten

Food prep

❑ **Picking and tearing (making a salad)**

Making a fresh salad is a fun project and can encourage your child to eat fresh veggies. Set out one or two types of lettuce and some fresh spinach, and let your child tear the greens into bite-sized pieces. If you are lucky enough to have something growing outside or in a pot that can be added—chives, herbs, green beans, or edible flowers, perhaps—have your child harvest, wash, and add it. Squeeze a lemon on top and drizzle some oil. Sprinkle some sunflower seeds or raisins on top, if you'd like.

❑ **Yummy ants and spiders**

Let your child create these delicious, fun snacks.

- Ants on a Log: Spread peanut or almond butter or cream cheese along the trough of a stick of celery. Dot the "log" with raisins or nuts).
- Pretzel Spiders: Spread nut butter on a round cracker, and press four pretzel stick "legs" onto each side. An almond or raisin can be used for the head. Dried cranberries or sunflower seeds can become spots on the spider's body.

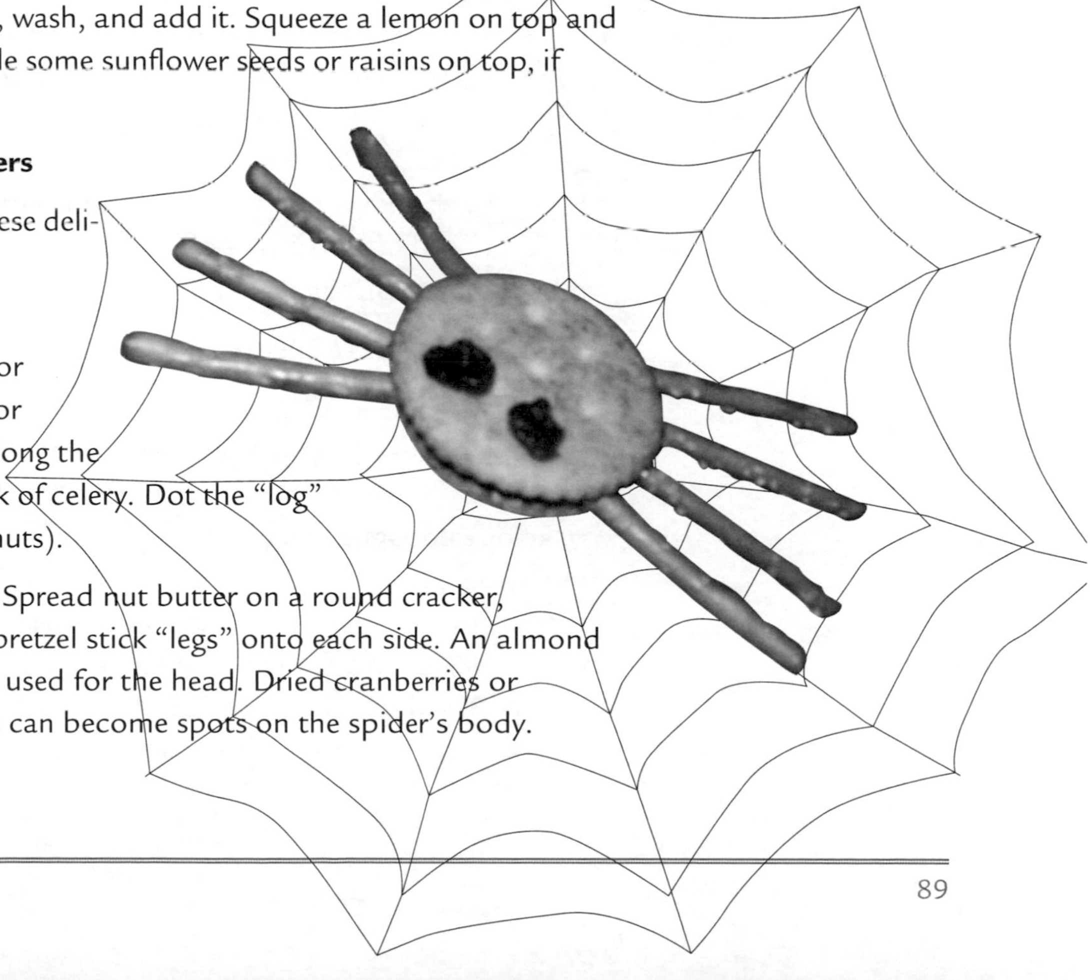

❑ **Washing and cutting (fruit salad)**

Ask your child to choose three to four types of fruit, such as an apple, a banana, an orange, and grapes. Demonstrate and supervise as your child washes the fruit, and then cuts it into bite-sized pieces. Place the fruit in a bowl and have your child gently toss it with hands or a spoon. This delicious snack can be eaten as is or with a spoonful of yogurt on top.

Grade 1 Baking

❑ **Count on the cook**

There is a lot of math in cooking. This activity is designed to help your child gain familiarity with making sense of all the numbers. Choose a simple recipe, such as banana bread, and read the recipe amounts with your child (or have your child read them to you). Discuss and practice measuring amounts with measuring cups (both dry and wet measure) and measuring spoons. Point out the oven temperature in the recipe and demonstrate setting the oven to preheat at the correct temperature. Once the recipe is assembled (let your child do as much as possible), demonstrate safe oven handling as you put the dish inside to bake. Consult the recipe again to see how long it should bake, and show your child how to set the timer. When the timer rings, show your child how to turn it off and safely remove the dish from the oven. Set the timer again if a cooling period is necessary before cutting or serving.

❑ **Bake your name**

Shaping bread dough is a wonderful experience. Prepare bread dough ahead of time (with or without your child's help) or use ready-to-bake pizza dough. When the dough has risen and is ready for shaping, show your child how to divide the dough into small balls about the size of your child's fist. Let your child sprinkle flour on the counter or in a baking tray (to keep it contained), and then demonstrate how to form the dough into a long snake. Show your child how to use the flour to keep the dough from sticking to hands or the surface. Shape each snake into a letter to spell out your child's name. You can also tie the dough into a loose knot to make a pretzel shape. Bake the dough letters or pretzels at 375 degrees for approximately 15 minutes (or until lightly browned).

❑ **Apple pancakes**

Apples make a wonderful addition to pancakes—they add nutrition and flavor at the same time. Allow your child to be the head chef for this activity (doing as much as possible) while you are the ever-ready assistant. First, have your child cut an apple into thin slices (you might have to do that part) and then chop it into small pieces. Prepare your favorite pancake batter, and then add the apples to it. Demonstrate pouring the batter into the pan (a ¼ cup measuring cup makes a good sized ladle), and let your child carefully pour the batter into the pan (watch out for splattering oil). You can flip the pancakes when they are ready.

Grade 2

Stovetop cooking

❑ **Making tea**

Making tea might seem extremely simple to adults, but there are several steps that a child will not automatically know how to do. Have your child write down the steps of the process while you dictate them. Remember to include details such as measure the amount of water you'll need, cover the pan so the water boils faster, and get out the cups and spoons while you wait for the water to boil. Provide instructions on how to turn the stove on and off (you'll supervise that part). Once everything is written down, supervise as your child follows the directions to prepare a cup of tea for you both. You will pour the boiling water into the cups, but your child can do everything else. Using an actual teapot, if you have one, can add a special touch of ceremony to this process.

❑ **Grilled cheese**

Making a grilled cheese sandwich is a very useful skill. Talk your child through the steps, but let him or her perform each task. You may want to flip the sandwich, or give careful instructions on how to do so without burning oneself. Have your child cut up an apple to accompany this meal.

❑ **Stew**

Making a soup or stew on the stove or in a crockpot is very satisfying. Help your child choose a recipe, assemble the ingredients, and prepare the food. Have your child start the stew in the morning and check it throughout the day. Involve your child in tasting the stew and adjusting the seasoning.

Grade 3
Making a meal

❑ **Choose three**

There are lots of wonderful cookbooks and recipes with just three ingredients. Find a book or ideas online, and let your child choose a three-ingredient recipe to make. Discuss and demonstrate food preparation and cooking techniques. Try to find recipes your child can handle without your help. Here are just a few:

- Quesadilla with tortilla, cheese, and beans
- Pasta with artichoke hearts and tomatoes
- Bread with apple slices and melted cheese on top
- Polenta rounds with pesto and tomato

Talk about the food groups that are included in your three-ingredient recipe.

❑ **Shopping trip and pantry stores**

Although your child has probably accompanied you to the grocery store for years, going food shopping when you are the chef is a very different experience. Have your child create a menu for a single dinner, or for a whole week of dinners. Help your child create a list of necessary ingredients, and then have your child check your pantry stores and check off ingredients that are already in the house. As you shop for the remaining ingredients, discuss food sources and options (see

"Choosing ingredients" in lesson 14). Involve your child in preparing and serving the meals from the menu plan.

❑ **Themed meal**

It can be great fun to plan a meal around a certain theme. It can be especially enjoyable to create a meal that relates to a place or time period that your child is studying in social studies or English literature. Let your child choose a theme, create a menu plan, make a shopping list, and cook the meal (with your help, of course). Meals can include a salad or appetizer, a main course, and a dessert. Here are some ideas to get you started:

- Pick a country (Mexico, Greece, Italy, Japan, etc.)
- Go USA (all the food has to be red, white, or blue)
- Book theme (make recipes from a favorite story or series)

Two wonderful recipe books with literary tie-ins are *The Redwall Cookbook* by Brian Jacques and *The Little House Cookbook: Frontier Foods from Laura Ingalls Wilder's Classic Stories* by Barbara Walter. (See the recommended reading list for details.)

Notes

Lesson 16 Exercise and Sleep

Exercise and sleep are just as important to the body as healthy food. Choose one (or more) of the following explorations around exercise and sleep.

Kindergarten

Sleeping and waking

❑ **Good morning**

How does your child wake up in the mornings? Does he or she come awake easily, ready for action, or wake up slowly and need a gentle morning routine? Many families have a regular bedtime routine but let the morning start with a less-than-organized jump into the day. Talk to your child about your morning routine and see if you can find ways to get your day off to a good start. For instance, a five minute morning stretching session or a ten-minute walk before breakfast can help set a relaxed, cooperative tone for the day. Come up with a few ideas for a morning routine, and try a new one each morning for a week. Discuss which ones worked well, and which ones didn't, and why.

❑ **Good night**

Ask your child, "What helps you fall asleep?" Tell your child what you do to fall asleep. Then have your child ask several other people, "What do you do to fall asleep?" Responses might include things like reading in bed, a foot massage, reviewing the good things that happened that day, a nighttime stretch and deep breathing, or curling up with a beloved cat or a favorite blanket or pillow. Find out if any of the responses sounds like something your child might like to try. Try something new each night for a week, and talk about what worked and what didn't.

❑ **Wind up and unwind**

Sometimes sleep cycles change and a child can have trouble falling asleep. Here's an activity to help the body relax and prepare for sleep. By first flexing and tensing muscles, it becomes easier to relax and, quite literally, unwind. Have your child lie in bed (on top of or under the covers). Ask your child to wind up or tangle together his or her fingers (cross them and twist them together in as many ways as possible). You do it, too. When you both have your fingers all wound up in a knot, hold them tight and count to five together, and then unwind and relax your fingers while taking a deep breath and blowing it out. Next, wind up your arms, curling them around one another, twisting and crossing them in any way you can manage. When your arms (and your child's) are all tangled up, hold them tight and count to five together. Unwind and release them while letting out a deep breath. Repeat with legs (and toes, if you can—challenging!). Afterwards, lie quietly for a minute, enjoying the satisfying sense of muscle release that comes after holding tension, and then continue with your regular bedtime story or routine.

Grade 1

Exercise anywhere, anytime

❑ **Room for everything**

Exercise doesn't need to take up a lot of space, and this activity helps prove it. Begin by using chalk (if you are outside) or tape or some other visual marker to create a box about four feet square. You and your child will take turns demonstrating active exercises that can be done in this space. For instance, you might leap from one side of the space to the other, or roll, cartwheel, or dance. You can do whatever you like, as long as you don't step outside of the box. After a few turns for each of you, change the size of the box to three feet square, and repeat. Perhaps you can still do some of the same things but have to modify your movements (taking higher leaps rather than long ones, for example). Try to come up with new ideas or variations. Next, reduce the size of the box to two feet square. What happens now? Can you still do energetic exercise? How about jumping jacks or squats? Finally, shrink the box to one foot square and explore active movement that keeps your feet in one spot (like jumping rope, hula hooping, or marching in place). Have fun with it!

❑ **We will have weather**

People exercise in all kinds of weather. Have your child draw pictures of three different outdoor exercises or activities that he or she likes to do when it is sunny. Next, draw pictures of three different outdoor exercises or activities that your child likes to do when it is rainy (you might have to help with some ideas of your own). Finally, draw three different pictures of outdoor exercises that can be enjoyed when it is snowy. Next, look outside to determine the weather, and choose one of the activities to do.

❑ **Big and small**

This is a silly game which brings attention to different kinds of movement. Begin by brainstorming a list of five full body activities (like running, climbing, jumping jacks, etc.). These should be activities that can be easily done in your house or yard. Write them down. Next, brainstorm five activities that use mainly the hands (fine motor control), like drawing, knitting, doing a puzzle, etc. Write them down. Now, have your child try to match up pairs of exercises that can be done simultaneously. You might find that all possible combinations are impossible (knitting while doing jumping jacks??) but you will have fun imagining the crazy combinations. Finally, choose one full body (large motor) activity and one fine motor activity to do before the day is over.

Grade 2
Understanding your body's needs

❑ **Body mechanics**

In this activity, you and your child will take turns moving one another's limbs to explore joints, muscles, and range of motion. Ask your child to stand still. Say, "Pretend you are my puppet and your body can only move if I move it." Begin by lifting your child's hand and turning it this way and that, and then putting it down. Move the arm to make it bend at the elbow, and then circle the shoulder joint. Your child will probably get the giggles—it feels funny to have someone else control your body!—but you can give a mock-serious reminder that "Puppets don't laugh!" (This will probably cause more giggles.) Move from arms and shoulders to legs and feet, lifting one at a time while keeping your "puppet" from falling. After you've enjoyed this for a while, switch places and you become the puppet while your child experiments with what joints and limbs can and can't do.

❑ **What happened?**

There are lots of body changes that occur during exercise, and this activity draws your child's awareness to these changes. Begin by having your child exercise vigorously for five minutes. When five minutes are up, have your child come to a stop and ask, "What does your body feel like?" If that doesn't elicit any specific responses, prompt more careful observations with questions like these:

- How fast is your heart beating?
- Is your forehead sweaty?
- Are you breathing harder than normal?
- Do your muscles feel tight or loose?
- Do you feel warm?

Have your child complete another five minutes of exercise and see if he or she comes up with any additional observations. Talk about why these changes occur.

❑ **Restful breaks**

While children often seem to go-go-go all day, finding ways to take a break from the action during a busy day can be very beneficial. Talk to your child about ways he or she likes to rest and take a break from being active during the day. Reading a book is often a preferred choice. See if you can come up with a list of several ideas. Consider creating a rest spot where your child can go for a peaceful break. Maybe there's a small nook where you can add pillows and a blanket, and a basket of books or an audio book set-up. Making a fort creates another good place to take a break. You can drape a sheet over the back of a couch or chair to make a quiet tent-like refuge.

Grade 3
Sleep schedule

❑ **Track your rhythms**

Have your child keep track of the amount of sleep time for one week. Create a chart to write down the time of waking and the time of going to sleep. Add a column for your child to calculate the number of hours spent sleeping per night. Include space for your child to write notes about the level of energy each day or the feeling of being tired. Talk about the sleep schedule and any changes that might need to be made to improve the quality or quantity of sleep.

❑ **Dream journal**

Writing down dreams or sharing them aloud can be a great experience. If your child doesn't usually remember dreams, this activity can help. Put a small notebook by the bed and have your child decorate the cover with the title Dream Journal. (This will help remind your child of the intention to remember and record dreams.) As soon as he or she wakes, have your child write down or tell any images or dreams that can be remembered. You can help by asking about the dream recollection as soon as you greet your child in the morning. Continue this for one week and see if your child's dream recall improves. You can do the activity yourself as well and share your dreams with your child.

❑ **Progressive relaxation**

Taking a few minutes at night to relax the body can promote a more restful sleep and an easier transition from waking to sleep. Here are two ways this can be done (both can be done after your child is in bed under the covers). Explain to your child how the exercise works before you begin. At first it will be helpful for you to lead the exercise by saying each step aloud, but if your child enjoys these exercises, he or she will quickly learn to do them without your help.

- Body Rest: Beginning with the toes, you will work your way through each part of the body, telling it to relax. Begin by saying, "Close your eyes and take a deep breath. Now tell your toes to relax. Toes, relax." Wait a few moments, and then continue: "Now tell your feet to relax. Feet, relax."
  Pause again, giving your child time to feel the feet relax. Sometimes it helps to wiggle the body part slightly and then let

it relax. Let your child know this is okay (sometimes the strain of trying to hold the body still creates more tension). Continue to slowly and quietly work your way through the body: "Relax, calves. Relax, knees." Talk your child through relaxing the thighs, hips, stomach, back, shoulders, arms, hands, fingers, neck, face, and, finally, eyes.

- Tense and Relax: This exercise is similar to the first one, but your child tenses each body part for a few seconds before relaxing it. Your instructions might sound like this: "Squeeze your toes as tight as you can. Tighter, tighter! Now let them relax completely." Wait a few moments, and then continue with the next body part, working your way from the feet to the head, until the entire body has been tensed and relaxed.

Lesson

Stress Management

No matter how hard we try to create a harmonious home for our families, life can get stressful at times. Children can feel the strain of this as keenly as adults, and can benefit from developing skills to recognize and deal with stress effectively.

Kindergarten

Getting outside

❑ Run for fun

Exercise is an excellent way to shake off the physical tension and negative feelings caused by stress. Running has its own element of sheer joy. Tell your child that the two of you are going to come up with a plan of where/how far to run when one of you needs a break or feels frustrated. Plan an easily accessible route: once around the outside of the house, for instance, or down the driveway to the mailbox and back, or around the backyard and up and down the steps three times. Practice the "Run for Fun" route when your child is in a good mood, and talk about using a phrase ("Time to run for fun!") when one of you needs a break.

❑ Dig and pour

Sensory activities, like playing in the sand, dirt, or water, have a very soothing effect. The next time your child is showing signs of stress (seems distracted, frustrated, angry, has a tense facial expression, etc.), introduce a sensory activity like one of the following:

- Put some sand in a plastic dishpan or baking tray with some glass "gems," small animals or vehicles, or small wooden blocks. (If your child doesn't immediately get involved, you can move a few things around and push the sand a bit with your finger to get things started.)

- Fill the sink with warm water, add a few drops of dish soap, and drop in an egg beater, whisk, and a couple of small plastic cups for pouring. A straw can also be used to blow bubbles (you might have to show your child how to do this).
- Take a shovel outside and dig up a small patch of dirt. Add a few toy cars, sticks, rocks, or blocks to encourage hands-on play.

Afterwards, when your child is feeling better, talk about how he or she felt before and after this sensory play. This is a good opening for a simple conversation about learning to recognize when you need a break and doing something that will help you feel more relaxed.

❑ **Walk out loud**

It's hard to hold on to stress when walking outside and talking, or better yet, singing. Take a hike together and start talking or singing, encouraging your child to do the same. When you see your child begin to relax, invite a conversation about handling stress by talking about your own experience. For instance, you might say, "Whenever I'm feeling tense about something, it always helps me to take a walk. I usually start feeling better right away, like a heavy weight is lifted off my shoulders, and I can take a deep breath and relax. Do you ever feel that way?" You don't have to try to bring your child's attention to it any more formally—just a simple conversation like this can help your child begin to develop effective stress management skills.

Grade 1
Figuring out what bothers you

❑ **Bother list**

A big part of learning to manage stress is learning to recognize what triggers it. This is different for each person, of course. Create a bother list with your child—one for each of you—listing all the things that bother each of you. Feel free to make suggestions for one another's list: "I notice that you don't like it when someone slams the door" or "I think it bothers you when your brother takes your toys without asking." Your child might want to illustrate his or her list. If you'd like, brainstorm solutions to managing these stressors in an effective way.

❑ **Stress continuum**

This activity can help your child begin to judge different levels of stress. Draw a line with chalk outside or place a tape measure or a long ribbon on the floor inside. On one end of the line, place a happy face, and on the other end, a sad face. Begin by mentioning something that bothers you and stand on the line in a place between happy and sad that illustrates how much this thing bothers you. For instance, you might say, "I don't like it when people leave their shoes in the middle of the floor. It bothers me this much," and go stand on the line about one-third of the way toward happy (closer to happy than sad, or wherever feels right to you). Take turns with your child saying something you don't like and moving to different points along the continuum.

Keep the focus on stress-producing scenarios and not opinions, such as food dislikes. If your child says, "I don't like broccoli," you can rephrase it to, "I don't like it when I have to eat broccoli for dinner." (Broccoli isn't stressful, but eating broccoli is.) Afterwards, discuss ways to minimize the stressors or come up with strategies to manage the ones that cannot change.

❑ **Count, sing, climb, and then check in again**

In this activity (which you can introduce either when your child is feeling relaxed and happy or when your child seems stressed), you'll encourage using a loud voice and large motor activities to diffuse the tension. The activity has three steps:

1. Acknowledge the need for a break.
2. Do a lively, noisy activity from the list below (or make up your own) for five minutes.
3. Check in again and report any change in feelings.

   Here are some good activities to try.

   - March around the house (inside or out) and loudly count 1-2-3-4 over and over, or chant a rhyme or sing a song in time to the marching. Demonstrate for your child big movements (high knees, arms swinging) and a very strong, loud voice.
   - Climb while singing a song—any song will do, or you can make up a silly song: "Look at me! I'm climbing in a tree!"

Climbing can take place in a tree (if you are lucky enough to have a good climbing tree), a climbing structure, or any sturdy obstacles in the house or yard. Even a step ladder will work, or your child can hop on and off of a chair. Set the timer for five minutes and encourage vigorous climbing and singing.

- Put on lively or dramatic music and dance while humming or singing along. Encourage big movements and loud vocal accompaniment. Dancing with a silk scarf can encourage large, sweeping motions.
- Use your hands to drum on your legs, making drumming sounds with your mouth at the same time. Or use your hands to drum on a table, wall, or a real drum, if you have one. Keep up a rhythm with your mouth that matches or complements the rhythm of your hands.
- Hand clapping (especially creating a complex rhythm) and tap dancing are also good ways to use the body as a percussion instrument. Remember to vocalize along with it.
- If you'd like, you can talk about how getting the heart and lungs pumping and the muscles flexing and active creates physical changes that help your mind and body to relax.

Grade 2

Relaxation techniques

☐ The great outdoors

Being outside in nature can have a relaxing effect that is almost instantaneous—you might notice deeper breathing, a calmer mind, and more relaxed movements within minutes (or even moments). Try several of these ways of being in nature over the next few days or weeks:

- Sit by a stream and listen
- Use a stick to draw in the dirt
- Try to silently follow a bird or squirrel
- Collect stones or sticks that look interesting
- Dig a hole in the sand and fill it up with water
- Wrap your arms around a tree and look up

Discuss with your child how each makes you feel. Does your body feel more relaxed? Do your thoughts feel calmer and clearer? Do you feel happy, or content, or peaceful?

❑ **Music and movement**

Music and movement go together naturally and most children will move their bodies to music without much prompting or guidance. Feel free to join in, though! Put on different types of music and play a couple of minutes of each type, such as pop, classical, rock, jazz, and folk. Talk about how you feel after moving in different ways to different music. Keep it simple: "That song made me feel like jumping." "That song made me think of lying in a hammock." Afterwards, you might discuss how relaxed you feel after dancing to music.

❑ **Visualization**

Many people use visualization to help them relax during times of stress. "Go to your happy place" has become a cliché for this technique, but the technique is quite valuable and very easy to teach to children. Explain to your child that visualization is helpful to do whenever he or she is feeling overwhelmed or anxious about something. It is fun to practice anytime, and practice will help your child be better able to draw upon his or her inner resources whenever needed.

Begin by asking your child to get in a comfortable position (sitting or lying down) with eyes closed. Say, "Take a deep breath, slowly breathing in through your nose, and then letting all the air out through your mouth." Do this for three or four breaths, and then ask your child to picture a place he or she really loves to be. Your child may want to talk about this place or just picture it silently. Encourage your child to picture this place in his or her mind as fully as possible, remembering as many details of how it looks, sounds, smells, and anything else that helps put the child in that imagined environment. At this point, you may begin to see a smile on your child's face as these happy memories work their magic. After your child has spent a few minutes imagining this favorite place, you might say something like, "You can open your eyes whenever you are ready, but remember you can always go back to this wonderful place whenever you need a little break from your worries." You can also suggest that your child might have several special places to call to mind to help him or her feel relaxed whenever it is needed.

Grade 3
When stress is good

❑ Motivating stress

There are times when stress can be beneficial. Many adults use short term stress motivators very effectively: deadlines or intense challenges (mental or physical) are good examples. This activity helps your child explore how stress can be useful in improving performance, which can lead to a lower level of anxiety-producing stress in the long run. When performance improves, you often feel better about yourself and feel better equipped to handle future challenges.

Begin this activity by asking your child to leap as far as possible. Mark the place where he or she took off and landed on the ground. Measure this if you'd like. Next, draw a line or place markers at the take-off and landing points and explain that your child has to jump again but this time cannot step on either line. You can be creative and say it is hot lava or an electric fence or a sleeping snake, or just say that under no circumstances must a foot touch either line. (This introduces tension into the situation.) Have your child leap again. Chances are good that the leap will be even further than the one that was "as far as possible." Talk about why this happened. You can explain how stress produces an adrenaline boost in the body, or just discuss how the situation made your child want to focus and try harder.

❑ Tension and relaxation

Tension can be detrimental if held in the body without being released, but tension can also lead to a greater sense of relaxation when it is released. Have your child try this (you do it, too) and talk about how relaxed the body feels after a period of extreme tension. Begin by having your child lie down on the floor and relax the legs. Ask your child to think about how the relaxed legs feel and remember this feeling. Next, do something very strenuous with the legs—a fast bike ride, running in place, running up and down stairs, etc. Do this strenuous activity for an additional 30 seconds or a minute longer than your child wants to—this is when the added level of tension comes in. Push your child to a greater effort just when energy is flagging. Act like a fitness trainer ("You can do it! Faster! Harder!"). Then walk for a minute or so until the heart rate and breathing are normalized, and then lie down again and have your child focus on relaxing the legs. Do they feel different now? More relaxed, or loose, or heavy? Warmer? Discuss what happened in the body as a result of pushing it into a state of tension and then fully releasing the tension.

- ❑ **Internal warning system**

  Recognizing stress, distinguishing helpful tension from anxiety-producing stress, and knowing when and how to release tension are important life skills. Brainstorm with your child ways to tell when stress is building up and what do what with the stress (use it or lose it). Every person will have different observations and ideas in this regard. Write down warning signs that the stress is not helpful or needs to be released, and include ideas for dealing with it.

Notes

Lesson 18

Unit III Review: Healthy Habits

Mark the activities you completed in the third unit (lessons 13–17). Explore in greater depth any topics in which your child was particularly interested or topics that you feel warrant a more detailed study. Revisit favorite activities or try a new activity that explores healthy habits.

Lesson 13: Nutrition

KINDERGARTEN	**Healthy food, clean water, fresh air** ❑ Fresh food ❑ Water, water everywhere ❑ Smell test
GRADE 1	**Balanced diet** ❑ I need/I want ❑ Keeping track ❑ The color plate
GRADE 2	**Six essential nutrients** ❑ What are the six essential nutrients? ❑ Favorites list ❑ Food group hopscotch
GRADE 3	**Weight management** ❑ Calories in/calories out ❑ Good fats, bad fats ❑ All filled up

Lesson 14: Food Choices

KINDERGARTEN	**Food groups** ❏ Food group faces ❏ Building a meal ❏ What do animals eat?
GRADE 1	**Food pyramids** ❏ Draw food pyramids ❏ Sweet is a treat ❏ Salty or sweet?
GRADE 2	**Building your food pyramid** ❏ What did I eat today? ❏ Draw your personal pyramid ❏ So many ways to eat healthy
GRADE 3	**Meal planning** ❏ Choosing ingredients ❏ Timing it right ❏ Something for everyone

Lesson 15: Enjoying Food

KINDERGARTEN	**Food prep** ❑ Picking and tearing (making a salad) ❑ Yummy ants and spiders ❑ Washing and cutting (fruit salad)
GRADE 1	**Baking** ❑ Count on the cook ❑ Bake your name ❑ Apple pancakes
GRADE 2	**Stovetop cooking** ❑ Making tea ❑ Grilled cheese ❑ Stew
GRADE 3	**Making a meal** ❑ Choose three ❑ Shopping trip and pantry stores ❑ Themed meal

Lesson 16: Exercise and Sleep

KINDERGARTEN	**Sleeping and waking** ❏ Good morning ❏ Good night ❏ Wind up and unwind
GRADE 1	**Exercise anywhere, anytime** ❏ Room for everything ❏ We will have weather ❏ Big and small
GRADE 2	**Understanding your body's needs** ❏ Body mechanics ❏ What happened? ❏ Restful breaks
GRADE 3	**Sleep schedule** ❏ Track your rhythms ❏ Dream journal ❏ Progressive relaxation

Lesson 17: Stress Management

KINDERGARTEN	**Getting outside** ❏ Run for fun ❏ Dig and pour ❏ Walk out loud
GRADE 1	**Figuring out what bothers you** ❏ Bother list ❏ Stress continuum ❏ Count, sing, climb, and then check in again
GRADE 2	**Relaxation techniques** ❏ The great outdoors ❏ Music and movement ❏ Visualization
GRADE 3	**When stress is good** ❏ Motivating stress ❏ Tension and relaxation ❏ Internal warning system

Notes

Lesson 19 Respect and Good Sportsmanship

This lesson focuses on the concepts of respect for self and others, and good sportsmanship. Be alert to the many instances in your child's day when respect and good sportsmanship can be noticed (and instances of disrespect and not being a good sport can be discussed). Choose one or more activities to complete, based on your child's interests, strengths, and challenges.

Kindergarten

Respect for self and others

❑ **Golden rule**

The Golden rule—Do unto others as you would have them do unto you (or, in plainer language, treat others the way you want to be treated)—can be useful in teaching children the meaning of respect. Have your child create and decorate a sign with the Golden Rule, and hang it up in your home. Your child can write the rule verbatim or use his or her own words. Use the rule as a discussion starter when issues of respect arise.

❑ **Is it fair?**

This is an activity that helps your child explore the issue of fairness. Present your child with questions like the following, and discuss how to create a solution that is fair to everyone.

- Three friends have a sleepover, but there are only two beds
- Five friends are hungry for snack, but there are only four oranges
- Two people are hungry but they

can only eat one at a time because there is only one place to sit (and they have to be sitting in order to eat).

Try to keep the discussion focused on fairness instead of veering toward mathematical solutions of equality (which are probably too advanced for your kindergartener, anyway). Fair doesn't necessarily mean equal and equal isn't always fair. For instance, if two people are hungry, it might make sense to flip a coin to see who eats first, but it would be more fair to let the hungrier person eat first, or the one who hadn't eaten for the longest time. The solutions of fairness should revolve around sharing, taking turns, considering the needs of others, etc.

❏ **Listening**

It can be frustrating to be interrupted when you are speaking to someone (in person or on the phone). Learning to listen and waiting to speak are wonderful skills to encourage in your child. Some households are naturally very talkative, in which case this listening activity can be especially useful. When there is an important discussion or one to which everyone wants to contribute, come up with a system to ensure everyone takes turns listening and speaking. You child can help devise (and enforce) this system. You might sit in a circle and go around the circle in order; you might speak in turn from the youngest to the oldest, or vice versa; you might use a talking stick or feather or some other token to pass around—only the person holding it can speak and everyone else has to listen.

Grade 1
Rules and fair play

❏ **Making the rules (and following them)**

Every game has rules and these rules must be followed by everyone playing the game. It doesn't matter what the rules are as long as everyone agrees to follow them. In this activity, your child will have the opportunity to make up a game's rules that everyone has to follow. You can help by suggesting a type of game, such as a race, tag, hide and seek, or a guessing game, and then guide your child in defining the rules. Here are some questions you can use to help your child clarify the parameters of a game of tag or a race (you can ask similar questions for other types of games).

Tag:

- How do you decide who is "it"?
- How long does this person count before beginning the chase?
- Where are the boundaries?
- Are any areas out of bounds?
- What happens when you get tagged (do you freeze, go to "jail," drop out of the game, become "it")?
- Does the game have an end or a winner?

Race:

- Where is the starting line, and where is the finish line?
- Who calls the start?
- How is the race started (by counting down from 3 to 1 and saying "go," by counting up from 1 to 3 and saying "go," by saying, "ready, set, go," etc.)?
- Is it a running race, a walking race, a hopping or skipping race?
- Do you have to stay in your "lane" or can you run in front of someone (for instance, when going around a corner)?
- Can you touch another runner?

The purpose of this activity is to help your child understand the rationale behind the rules and to become invested in upholding the rules—making up the rules makes your child the expert on the rules of that particular game. Learning to respect the rules is part of learning how to play fair.

❑ **You be the judge**

Being the one who decides the outcome of a contest or a disagreement is not easy. Let your child be the judge the next time there is a game with a winner (like a race) or a contest, or a simple judgment call regarding fairness. You may find your child is naturally diplomatic in issuing a verdict, or that your child needs some guidance from you in coming to a decision or in communicating it to others with sensitivity.

❑ **Equal vs. fair**

Ask your child to explain the difference between equal and fair. These two concepts are often confused by children. If this is the case, you can help your child understand the difference by offering the following scenarios for discussion:

- Two people are hiking. One is very hungry, but the other one is not hungry at all. They find two ripe apples on a tree. Who should get the apples? What is equal? What is fair?
- Three people are taking a wheelbarrow full of watermelons to the market. It is very heavy and hard to push. Two of the people are adults and one is a child. They have a 30-minute walk to the market. Should they each take turns pushing the heavy load? What is equal? What is fair?

You can come up with other situations, or use a real-life situation to further illustrate the difference between equal and fair.

Grade 2
Good sportsmanship

❑ Win or lose with a smile

Find a game your child likes to play, preferably one that is short (so you can play multiple times). Card games work well since several hands are often played in one sitting; tic-tac-toe is another good, quick game. You may be in the habit of letting your child win frequently, but learning to lose gracefully is an important skill (and one you have probably modeled on numerous occasions). Play the game with your child, taking turns with who wins. If your child is a gracious winner or loser, make a point of noticing his or her good sportsmanship, mentioning specifics. Define *sportsmanship* if it is unfamiliar to your child. If your child gets grumpy when losing or gloats when winning, take the opportunity to talk about how important it is to be a good sport. You might suggest a few simple behaviors your child can emulate, such as making eye contact and congratulating the opponent on a good game. Helping your child acknowledge how nice it feels to win can lead to a more cheerful attitude when your child loses. You might point out how easy it is to feel appreciation for the winner's skill or good fortune, or emphasize how easily a sore loser can spoil the sense of fun and accomplishment felt by the winner.

❑ Keeping score

Find a game your child likes to play for which you normally keep score, such as tennis, basketball, ping-pong, etc. Play one game without keeping score, explaining to your child that all the rules are the same but you'll be playing for fun, and not to keep track of who scores the most points and wins. Play for a set amount of time (say, ten minutes)—you may have to remind your child, or yourself, not to keep track of points aloud or in your head. After the time is up, start the game over and this time keep score. When the game is over, ask your child if it felt different to play without keeping score. If so, why? This is a good way to begin a conversation about competiveness, cooperation, and good sportsmanship.

❑ **Beginner's luck**

Ask your child to choose a favorite game to teach to someone who has never played before. Your child can teach someone younger, older, or the same age. You might want to give a few pointers about helping a beginner, such as the following:

- Explain the rules first but expect to have to give frequent reminders.
- Let the beginner have more than the usual number of chances to win since he or she will just be learning the skills and strategy.
- Explain your moves as you play or breakdown technique into step-by-step instructions.
- Be encouraging even if the beginner is not very good at the game.

Part of good sportsmanship is the willingness to pass along skills and tips to those just starting out. Rather than keep knowledge and technique secret in order to maintain a competitive edge, a good sport will share the love of the game with whoever is interested.

Grade 3
Dealing with disrespect

❑ **What would happen if...?**

It is possible that your child will have to deal with being treated disrespectfully at some point in life. This activity uses role playing in a safe environment to allow your child to practice how to respond effectively. Explain that you'll be taking turns pretending to be someone who is disrespectful, rude, or unkind, and the other person has to respond.

Begin by asking your child to play the role of the disrespectful person, and to cut in front of you as you stand in line somewhere (you can pretend to be waiting your turn at a slide, waiting in line for tickets at the movies, or anything that your child will be familiar with). Model behavior you'd like your child to display, such as a polite reminder, "Excuse me, I was in line first." The next stop, if the rude behavior continues, depends a great deal on your values. You might want to yield and drop the matter, report it to someone in charge, or continue to apply verbal pressure as you stand up for yourself. Other scenarios could include crowding someone out of their space on a bench; taking a toy without asking and refusing to give it back, giving an insult under the guise of teasing; or not letting others have a turn. Model behavior for your child and then switch places and let your child show you how to respond to disrespect.

❑ **Agree to disagree**

There are often times when people disagree, and disagreeing with respect is an important skill to cultivate. Find a topic about which you and your child disagree, or tell your child you'll each choose one side of an issue to debate. Explain that the goal is to disagree with one another strongly while still behaving with respect. This includes not only avoiding disrespectful words but also rude body language, such as making faces, eye rolling, contemptuous noises, finger pointing, or other gestures that can seem dismissive or insulting. Argue for a while, making sure to follow the rules of decorum yourself and to point out any infractions by you or your child. End the exercise by agreeing to disagree and shaking hands.

- [ ] **Stand up for your rights**

In this activity, your child gets to practice assertive language to use when not being treated fairly. Ask a series of questions like the ones below and have your child speak up for him- or herself in a clear, strong, respectful voice. Possible responses are given for the first two—you might need to prompt your child's response by modeling clear language.

What would you say if…

- you were in a group and everyone else's opinion was listened to except for yours?

  (You might say, "I'd like to give my opinion, too.")

- someone was handing out a free toy to everyone in the group except to you?

  (You might say, "I noticed everyone got a free toy. If there are any left, I'd like to have one, too.")

- everyone was taking turns in a game but someone said that you couldn't have a turn?
- the group was voting on what to do next and everyone got to have a vote except for you?

Notes

Lesson 20 Social Skills

Friends often make up a good portion of our social circles and support networks. Having strong social skills can help us make and keep friends. Social skills are developed throughout life, and these activities help your child focus on the many ways to develop social intelligence.

Kindergarten

Making friends

❑ **Friend card**

Good friends enrich our lives and should always be appreciated. One way to do that is to celebrate friendships. Ask your child to name one special friend and to create a card for that friend. This can be a "Thank you for being such a good friend" card or an "I like being friends with you" card, or anything along those lines. Have your child draw a picture of something the friend likes, or a picture of him or her and the friend doing something fun together. Deliver the card in person or send the card in the mail for a lovely surprise.

❑ **Friend pyramid**

On a large piece of paper, draw a small circle at the top and center of the paper, and write your child's name inside. This is the peak of the pyramid. Ask your child to name as many friends as he or she can think of, draw circles underneath your child's name, and put each of these names inside. Connect these circles to your child's circle by drawing a line between them. Next, have your child help you count up the number of friend circles, and then add the same number of additional circles below to each friend's name, representing all the other friends each one is likely to have. For example, if your child names three friends, the top level of the pyramid would have one circle (your child's), the second level would have three circles (the three friends), and the third level would have nine circles (the friends' friends).

Have your child color in all the name circles—circles for your child, the friends, and the friends' friends—with many different colors. You might mention how wonderful it is for there to be so many friends in the world, and how each member of your family could make a similar picture with lots and lots of friend circles. This visual representation can convey (without you having to comment on it) the wonderful possibilities of friendship.

❑ **It's your turn**

Taking turns may be something at which your child is already quite good, or may be something with which your child needs more experience. In either case, this is a fun activity in which taking turns is an integral part. Get a piece of paper and cut it in half lengthwise, so you have a tall, thin rectangle. Tell your child that you are going to draw a funny creature together, each taking a turn adding something new. You can begin by drawing a silly head shape, and then say, "It's your turn," and tell your child to draw the next part—maybe funny arms (several) or crazy hair. Continue adding to the picture a little at a time, always taking turns (not drawing at the same time) and waiting patiently while the other person draws. When your crazy creature is complete, your child may want to add color. Use the second piece of paper to take turns drawing another crazy creature.

Grade 1
Personal space

❑ **Space bubbles**

This game underscores the concept of personal space. It works best with several people. Begin by drawing a series of chalk circles on the ground, each circle about a foot in diameter and nearly touching its neighbors. Each circle needs to be large enough to stand inside, and the circles should be close enough to step easily from one to the next. (Alternately, you can place circles of paper on the floor, making sure they are placed close together.) Use at least one more circle than the number of players (if you have three players, place four circles on the floor). Each person chooses a circle to stand on. The object of the game is for everyone to move from circle to circle until they have stepped on each circle at least once. This has to be done without touching another person, and you can't step on a circle that someone else is already on. This game may lead to a fit of giggles as everyone bends and twists while trying to move from circle to circle without getting in each other's space.

❑ **How small is your house?**

This activity is a good way to help your child become aware of the sense of personal space. Take a bed sheet and help your child build a small fort using a table, chairs, or couch. Once it is built, crawl inside with your child, saying you are pretending to be foxes in their den. Try to get comfortable, finding enough space for each of you. Stay there for a few minutes, and then climb out and tell your child that now you'll be rabbits, so you need to make your house a bit smaller. Push the sides of the fort closer (rearrange the sheet, if necessary, so it isn't sagging), and crawl inside again. Make your rabbit selves as comfy as possible. You and your child may be feeling a little cramped—that's good! After a few minutes, crawl out again and say now you'll turn into mice. Make the house very small and try to fit inside once more. All your limbs might not fit, but that's okay. After trying to make it work, crawl out and reset the fort to human size. Talk about how each person needs a certain amount of space to feel comfortable.

❑ **Too close, too far**

This is an activity that explores how close people need to be for different kinds of talking. First, stand a normal distance apart and talk to one another—you might just say, "Hi, how are you? What's your name?" Speak in a normal tone of voice and begin backing up slowly (make sure there's nothing behind you to bump into). Keep talking a normal voice until it is hard to hear one another. You can go into another room, if you are indoors. Once you are so far apart that normal speaking doesn't work, begin shouting your conversation. Keep yelling to one another as you begin moving towards each other. Keep your voices raised until you are standing a few feet apart. Then drop your voice and begin whispering very, very quietly. Start moving toward one another, still whispering, until you are face to face. Then begin speaking in a normal voice again and back up until you are a comfortable distance apart for normal speaking. Ask your child what it felt like to yell when you were standing close together, or to speak normally when your faces were very close to one another, or to be too far apart to hear normal speech.

Grade 2

Stand on your own two feet

❑ **Go your own way**

Take a hike in the woods and at every opportunity where you see an option or choice, stop and point it out to your child: "I'm going to walk around this big rock. You can walk around it, too, or you can climb over it." Your child can choose. You can also give your child a choice and then you choose the other option: "Do you want to go over this fence or climb under it? Okay, I'll go the other way." These simple experiences of independent choice and action help build a sense of self-reliance and trust in one's own abilities.

❑ **Marching to your own drummer**

As Shakespeare said, "To thine own self be true." Being true to yourself or marching to your own drummer is literally played out in this activity. Find two things to drum on (drums, pots, table, knees, etc.) and use hands, sticks, chopsticks, or drumsticks. Have your child start a simple beat and you join in to reinforce a steady rhythm. When your child is drumming confidently, begin drumming a different beat while your child maintains the original rhythm. Do that for a minute, rejoining the original rhythm if your child falters. End by drumming in unison again. Then repeat the process with a new rhythm that you maintain while your child beats a different rhythm. If you'd like, you can talk about it afterwards, relating it to how sometimes you want to join in with what others are doing and sometimes you want to do your own thing.

❑ **Would you do what Simon says?**

Play a game of Simon Says to help your child identify limits and know when to say no. Begin the game with simple things you know your child can do, and then give a wildly impossible task, like "Simon

Says fly up to the sun." The goal is for your child to say, "I can't do that!"(although he or she might try to act it out for fun). Continue the game with normal challenges, and then give another impossible task, like, "Simon Says turn straw into gold" or "Simon Says chop down a tree with your hands." This is meant to be done in a playful manner while encouraging your child to know when to refuse to do something beyond his or her limits or beyond reasoning.

Grade 3

Dealing with bullying, teasing, and threats

❑ **Bad words, bad feelings**

This dramatic role playing game uses stuffed animals to help your child begin to understand the feelings behind bullying and threats. Find a stuffed animal (one that isn't your child's favorite is probably best) and tell your child to pretend to be mean to the stuffed animal by saying mean things. Your child might say things like, "You're ugly. I hate you. You are stupid. You can't do anything right." Next, ask your child how that felt inside to say those terrible things. He or she will probably report feeling awful. Let your child apologize and make up with the stuffed animal (he or she will probably want to!)—this allows your child to release any lingering negative feelings. Then have a discussion about how a bully or someone acting mean might feel awful inside and how these feelings might lead to this person acting in unkind ways.

❑ **Was that nice?**

Teasing can be fun and funny, but it can easily cross the line into being hurtful. In order to help your child determine when teasing is friendly and when it's not, have him or her keep a list of all the teasing remarks overheard in a day. Ask your child to write them down and add a note about how the remark was received. Your child might need help determining which overheard remarks qualify as teasing, such as, "Here comes trouble!" or "Late again? We're going to start calling you Mr. Turtle." When the list has several entries, discuss which ones were fun for the recipient and which may have caused discomfort, regardless of how well-intended. Explain that the oft-heard defense of "I was only joking" doesn't excuse making someone else unhappy or uncomfortable.

This activity can easily lead into an excellent introduction to the art of making a sincere apology. A sincere apology doesn't include the word "but." A sincere apology is one that takes full responsibility without making excuses for the behavior. Encourage your child to be specific when making an apology: "I'm sorry that what I said hurt your feelings," or "I'm sorry for turning the light off even though I knew you were still in the room."

❑ **Go wild**

When certain animals are threatened, they will make themselves look bigger and fiercer to ward off the attacker. They may stand as tall as possible, make eye contact, and growl. Other animals face a threat by rolling up in a ball and looking small and defenseless. In this activity, you will play act two scenes. In the first scene, you are a lion threatening a strong animal, such as another lion (played by your child). Roar and growl and pretend to charge at one another. In the second scene, you are a lion threatening a timid animal, such as a hedgehog (also played by your child). You'll roar and growl and charge while your child curls into a small, frightened ball. Afterward, ask your child how it felt to respond to a threat in a strong way and in a timid way. Next, reverse roles (your child threatens and you react in the two very different ways), and then ask your child how it felt to the "bully" when the target stood up for itself or when it rolled up and lay still. If you'd like, translate this metaphor into human terms and discuss real life scenarios.

Lesson

Communication Skills

Learning to communicate our needs is vital to health. Communicating our thoughts, dreams, goals, opinions, and ideas can be just as vital. This lesson helps develop communication skills through a wide variety of experiences.

Kindergarten

Talking through problems

❑ **1- 2- 3 Problem solving**

The next time your child comes to you with a problem, introduce this 1-2-3 problem solving technique. This consists of asking three questions:

1. What is wrong?
2. What do you wish?
3. What should we do?

Encourage your child to be very specific for answering question #1, and to think very creatively for question #2 (anything goes). Guide your child in coming up with realistic, practical steps for question #3. Once the practical steps start being considered, redefining #2 might be in order. Assist your child in coming to a satisfactory conclusion. Here is an example:

1. What is wrong? Jack wants to play in the sandbox but I want to swing.
2. What do you wish? I wish Jack wanted to swing. I wish Jack would do what I want all the time.
3. What should we do? We should take turns with who gets to decide what we'll do. We'll play in the sandbox for a while, and then go swing.

❑ **Striking a bargain**

Negotiating is an essential part of problem solving when it involves conflicting interests. While parents may not want to encourage negotiating with their children on most issues at home (where firm parental guidance still holds sway), let your child strike a bargain with you on a minor matter. You might negotiate about what game to play or what book to read next. Guide your child in the subtle art of give and take that is at the heart of negotiating skills. Instruct and model the willingness to compromise so that both parties get something they want.

❑ **Solutions instead of blame**

Children (and sometimes adults) are often quick to blame others when something goes wrong, such as when a toy gets broken, a cup gets spilled, or an item is lost. Be on the lookout for something like this—you probably won't have to wait long. There might be a light left on in an empty room, muddy footprints on the floor, or some other small thing that needs to be put to rights. Draw your child's attention to it by saying, "Look at that! What should we do about it?" If your child answers by finger pointing and saying, "I didn't do it! It's not my fault" or blaming someone else, just calmly reply, "I didn't ask who was responsible, but what we should do about it." The goal is to focus your child's attention on solutions rather than blame. If your child continues to insist that someone else is to blame and should take care of it, respond with, "Well, we're here now and it needs to be fixed, so what do we need to do?" or "We can all work together to fix it. What should we do first?" Each time someone points a finger and tries to lay blame (warranted or not), try to shift the focus to fixing the problem. Taking responsibility for actions is important, of course, but this activity gives your child the tools to move beyond blame to solutions.

Grade 1
Being a good listener

❑ **Do you hear what I hear?**

Find a place to go where you will hear many different sounds. Outdoors often works very well. Stand together with your child, and close your eyes and listen. Take turns identifying as many sounds as you can. Try this in another spot, maybe inside the house. Focus on sharpening your listening skills. The goal of this simple activity is to encourage your child to be an attentive listener. Listening is an essential social skill, and you might discuss how important it is to listen when others speak.

❏ **Find the word**

To encourage active listening (really paying attention to what you are hearing), you will have your child choose an unusual word, such as *artichoke* or *zebra*. Explain that you will tell a story and slip this word in somewhere, and after you are finished with your story, it is your child's job to identify where and how the word was used. Begin to spin a tale in which the key word is incidental, not an important part of the story. For instance, you might tell a story about a farmer going to market to sell a horse, and in the market he sees many types of fruits and vegetables (including artichokes), or your story might be about someone who builds a big house and puts all sorts of wild furnishings, such as a zebra-striped pillow on a revolving couch made out of thick pink fuzzy fake fur. Try hard to slip in the word unnoticed. You want your child to have to listen very closely to find the word, but he or she can't make a sound or show that the word has been used until the story is over. Continue the story for a bit after including the key word. After your story ends, ask your child how the word was used. If your child is interested, you can switch places and do it again, with you choosing a word and becoming the active listener.

❏ **What did I say? What did I mean?**

We often don't say exactly what we mean, and as a result, misunderstandings can arise. In this activity, you'll take turns making statements and discussing the various meanings behind the words. Here are some examples:

- "I want to go to the store" might really mean "I want to buy some milk."
- "I'm not hungry" might really mean "I don't want to eat what you are offering."
- "I don't feel like playing" might really mean "I don't want to play with you right now," or, "I want to play alone for a while."

Children can be overly focused on words, often taking things very literally, while using language themselves in a general, unspecified way. While we can't expect a first grade child to use language in a sophisticated manner, this activity can help focus your child's attention on the importance of trying to understand one another, regardless of how an idea or emotion is communicated.

Grade 2

Self-advocacy (how to get what you need)

❑ **Strong vs. loud**

Using a firm, strong voice communicates a sense of conviction and confidence, which is an important ingredient in self-advocacy. However, children often mistake a loud voice for a strong voice. A good way for children to practice using a firm voice without resorting to yelling is to work on dog training. If you don't have a dog, borrow one from a friend. Have your child put the dog through its tricks—most dogs know the commands to sit, shake, and lie down. Many dogs will cheerfully ignore a command unless it is given in a firm, confident tone of voice. Make sure to supervise your child to make sure the dog is treated properly and that your child is safe with the dog. Have your child reward the dog with a pat or praise when it responds to the command. Remind your child to continue speaking in a firm voice if the dog is not compliant (your child should not resort to yelling, tugging, or hitting). Demonstrate the correct way to give a firm command without raising your voice.

❑ **Asking instead of complaining**

This activity focuses on the difference between a complaint and a request. Some parents give the reminder, "Ask nicely," to prompt a child to rephrase a complaint into a request (such as "I never get a turn to pick the movie" to "May I please choose the movie tonight?"). In this game, your child will play the adult while you whine and complain. Your child will suggest polite rephrasing that you can use for each complaint you come up with. The following examples give you a few ideas:

- I don't like to wear that red shirt ⇨ May I choose another shirt to wear?
- That's too hard, I can't do it ⇨ I need help, please.
- You're always busy. You never play with me ⇨ When will you have time to play a game together?

❑ **What do I really want?**

Sometimes it's hard to pinpoint exactly what we want. This activity gives your child a chance to consider ways to articulate wants more clearly. Ask your child the true intent behind statements like the following. Sample responses are included to give you an idea of how you might need to prompt your child to be more specific.

Grade 3
Nonverbal communication

❑ **Body talk**

Learning to pay attention to nonverbal communication will help your child be a more effective communicator. Using two stuffed animals that are soft-bodied and easy to manipulate, have a conversation with the animals that is punctuated with lots of physical expression. You will control one animal and your child will control the other. Have your animals jump for joy, act puzzled, become sad, act eager, get mad, kiss and make up, get sleepy, etc., depending on the conversation. Have fun with it and see how many ways you can move your animal's body to express emotions that match the conversation.

What do you really want when you say:

- I'm not ready to go to bed. ⇨ I want to stay up ten more minutes.
- I'm hungry. ⇨ Can I please have a snack?
- I don't like that game. ⇨ I'd rather play something else.
- I can't sit still. ⇨ I'd like a break to run around.
- My tower keeps falling down.
- I can't do it.
- I'm bored.
- I feel lonely.

❑ **Charades**

The classic game of charades offers wonderful opportunities to use body language and facial expressions to give and receive clues. Enjoy a game with the whole family.

❑ **Model conversations**

If you have a magazine or newspaper with ads in it featuring models, this silly game can encourage your child to tune in to nonverbal communication. Choose a photo and take turns saying funny things that the models might have been thinking or feeling when the picture was taken, based on their postures, surroundings, and facial expressions. For instance, you might say, "I am really worried about how my grass is turning yellow," or "I love to walk in the rain!" or "This dress is so uncomfortable. I can't wait to change into my yoga pants." This is all in fun, but it also requires a keen eye toward expression.

Lesson 22

Mentors and Elders

All of us, young and old, need the support of mentors at some point in our lives, and every member of a community is important and vital to that community's health and success. This lesson focuses on identifying and appreciating your child's and your family's support system, particularly the mentors and elders, and on learning how to be an active community member, one that both gives and receives support within the community.

Kindergarten

Family and friends

❑ **Who do you love?**

Understanding the role, importance, and extent of a support system begins by recognizing all the people in your life who want to help you. Ask your child to start naming all the people he or she loves: family, relatives, friends, etc. Make sure to include people of all ages. The list may be long or short. Next, have your child draw a picture that uses flowers or trees or birds or hearts—whatever your child likes—to represent each person named (one image per person). You can write a name inside each flower, tree, bird, or heart, if you wish, and then display this picture in your child's room.

❑ **Teach me how**

In this activity, you'll begin by talking to your child about the things he or she has learned from family members or friends. Perhaps an uncle taught your child a funny song, a friend taught your child a new card game, and a sister taught how to braid hair or ride a bike. Your child has learned many, many things and there's a good chance that many people have acted as mentors. After you've spent some time reminiscing about the many people who have taught something, see if your child can come up with something he or she wants to learn, and who might be able to teach that. If possible, facilitate making this happen.

- ❑ **Family tree**

  Making a family tree using photos can help children get a strong sense of support and connectedness. Collect photos of each member of the family tree for three generations, if possible: your child's, yours, and your parents' generation. Your child can help cut out the faces of each person while you create a genealogical tree template that places your child's photo in a prominent position (top center or bottom center, for instance). Attach the photos and draw lines to show relationships. Label each photo with a name. Tell stories about each person as you create your family tree.

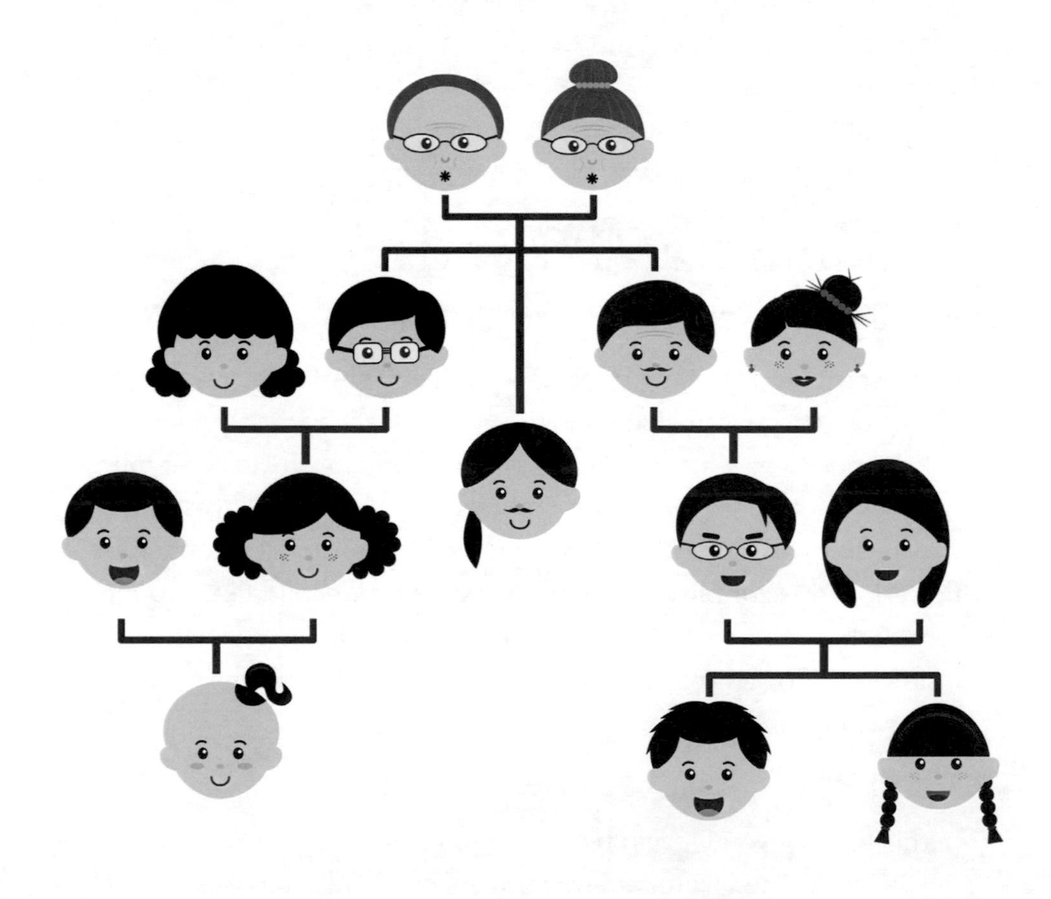

Grade 1
Circle of support

❑ From near to far

Is your extended family close-knit but far-flung? This activity creates a visual reference for how widespread your support system is. Begin with a blank map of the U.S. (or the world, if you have an international reach). You can copy a map by hand or print one off the Internet. The map should show the states in outline but not colored in. Have your child name all relatives he or she can think of one by one, and you point to where they live. Your child will color in that state. (You can get fancy and color-code the map—states with cousins in red, grandparents in green—or just let your child choose random colors.) When your child runs out of names, you continue the list until all the relatives are accounted for and their states are colored in. Next, move on to close family friends, if you'd like, and add them to the map.

❑ Friends chain

In this activity, friendships are celebrated by making a paper chain of children holding hands and having your child color each child differently. If you'd like, your child can assign a friend's name to each person on the chain and you can help your child write the names on each link. To make a person-shaped paper chain, follow these instructions (or look online for a simple template):

1. Fold a large piece of paper in half lengthwise and cut along the fold.
2. Fold each rectangle into an accordion fold approximately two inches wide.
3. Draw the half-profile of a person (head, one arm, and one leg), making sure to leave the paper intact at the fold at the hands and feet.

4. Carefully unfold the paper (your child will enjoy doing this part).
5. Tape or glue several chains together to make the chain as long as you'd like.

❑ **Rock-solid friends**

If you have room in your garden, this is a lovely way to celebrate your friendships. Collect as many stones as you can find that are relatively flat and about the size of your palm. You can also purchase these in a craft store or a garden center. Have your child wash them and set them out in the sun to dry. Assemble paints (acrylic or craft paints) and have your child think about designs to paint. Each rock will have the name of one friend (you'll probably want to paint that) and a colorful border or design (painted by your child). Encourage your child to include friends of all ages. Once all the rocks are painted and set out to dry, help your child choose a spot in the garden to display them. You can place these friend rocks in a circle around a tree trunk, bordering a flower bed, around the inside rim or the foot of a flower pot, or wherever you'd like.

Grade 2

Death is a part of life

❑ **Oldest person you know**

Ask your child, "Who is the oldest person you know?" Your child may have a good idea of who this is, or may not be very aware of relative age. If you can, get together with this person or with someone else who is elderly, and have your child ask, "What was it like when you were my age? What did you like to do when you were a child?" Listening to stories from the past is an excellent way to gain knowledge, insight, and perspective.

❑ **What to do when someone dies**

There may come a time when someone close to you passes away and your child becomes involved, however distantly, with the events that take place when a person dies. You might want to talk to your child about this process before it happens. You can explain, in as little or as much detail as you deem appropriate, what happens to the physical body when a person dies. You may want to talk about the person's spirit as well, depending on your spiritual beliefs. Then, you can talk about the different things the living do after someone passes away:

a memorial service or funeral, burial of the body or treatment of the ashes, sympathy notes or remembrance cards, etc. All this activity is often combined with strong emotions, grief as well as love and a sense of closeness shared by those who gather. Hearing about these things beforehand may make everything feel a little less confusing to your child when there's a death in the family.

❑ **Feelings about death**

Death brings on a wide range of emotions, and everyone has a unique emotional response to death. Has your child had a pet that died? Has someone close to your family died? Even the death of a favorite tree or a plant that was carefully tended can be difficult. Have a conversation about how it felt to experience this death. If you don't have something in your immediate environment which your child can relate to regarding death and loss, visit the library to find a storybook with a death theme (your librarian will probably have a good suggestion). The goal is to help your child understand that everyone reacts to death differently and there is no right or wrong way to feel.

Grade 3
Lending support to others

❑ **Who needs help?**

While there are probably many people you and your child can turn to for help, there are also many people whom you and your child might be able to help. Have your child choose two or three people you know and ask if they need help with anything. Your child might make some suggestions of different types of assistance, such as the following:

- move boxes
- wash car
- rake leaves
- walk dog
- weed garden
- pick fruit

- shovel snow
- pick things up at the grocery store

Afterward, talk with your child about how it feels to help others.

❑ **I'm good at...**

Help your child take stock of his or her skills and interests. Have your child make a list of things he or she is good at. No skill is too small. Is your child a good listener? Write that down. Able to play the piano? Write that down. Good at crossword puzzles, or building with blocks, or recognizing bird songs? Have your child write everything down. Next, help your child brainstorm ways to help others by sharing these abilities. Good at crossword puzzles? Maybe your great-grandmother loves them and you can do one together. Good at building with Legos? Maybe the neighbor's child loves Lego building and you could spend some time with the child to give the mother a break. Able to recognize bird songs? You might be a great guide for hikes. Help your child think of creative ways to use his or her talents, now and in the future.

❑ **Good Deed Day**

Declare a Good Deed Day! You and your child will spend the day performing acts of kindness for others. These can be small or large, anonymous or recognized. Another option is to decide that every Friday will be Good Deed Day, when you'll do one good deed for someone else.

Lesson

Anger Management

Even people who love one another very much get angry at one another at times. Negative emotions, such as anger, are a natural part of being human, and learning to deal with anger effectively is an essential part of growing up.

Kindergarten

How to show your anger

❑ **Angry body**

Children know what anger feels like, but they might not understand how it is expressed in the body. Choose a time when your child is in a good mood, and ask him or her to make a mad face (you make one, too). Next, ask him or her to show what angry hands looks like (or what you do with your hands when you are angry). Then ask to see angry feet. Ask to see an angry walk. You might even ask to see angry eyebrows or angry hair (that should be funny!). Finally, ask what an angry body looks like. Depending on how your child feels at this point (dissolving into giggles or becoming tense) you might de-escalate things by having your child show happy face, happy hands, happy feet, etc.

❑ **Mad words, mean words**

Most of us have had the experience of speaking in anger and saying something mean-spirited or hurtful. In this exercise, you will help your child begin to differentiate between mad words (words expressing feelings of anger) and mean words (words that are insulting or hurtful). There's a big difference. Ask, "What would you say if you were mad at someone for breaking your favorite toy on purpose?" Depending on the response, you can point out that these words express feelings clearly in a perfectly acceptable way, or that they are hurtful words. If hurtful, explain why they hurt, and help your child find a more appropriate way to express these strong emotions. Give your child a few different scenarios to help you discuss healthy ways to express anger verbally.

❑ **Mad art**

Expressing anger nonverbally through art—drawing, painting, music, dance, etc.—can be very helpful, especially to a young child whose verbal skills may not yet be very sophisticated. The next time your child is angry, guide him or her into a vigorous artistic activity. Choose one to which your child is naturally drawn. Instruct your child to "Draw your anger," or "Draw how that makes you feel." Afterwards, you might want to talk about how the child felt before and after the artistic activity.

Grade 1

How do I really feel?

❑ **So many emotions**

It's easy for many of us (both children and adults) to fall into the habit of identifying just a handful of emotions to describe the many ways we feel. We might say we're happy when we are really content or proud or blissful. We might say we're angry when we are really disappointed or frustrated or feeling betrayed. In this activity, your child will keep track of all the different feelings experienced over the course of one day or one week. You will need to help by reminding your child to write things down or by doing it yourself. The idea is not to interrupt your child's experience repeatedly but to help draw attention gently to the wide range of nuanced feelings experienced regularly in life. Help your child pinpoint an elusive or complex emotion by providing new feeling words.

❑ **That makes me feel...**

In this activity, your child will create a visual barometer of emotions. On strips of paper or small cards, write down as many emotions as your child can think of, one per strip. Have your child create a sign that says, "I'm feeling_____." Put the sign on your child's bedroom door or on the refrigerator (or wherever makes sense). Attach a small piece of rolled tape or double stick tape to the back of each emotion card, and place these in a long row beside the sign. Whenever your child recognizes a change in emotion, he or she can choose the appropriate emotion card and use it to fill in the blank.

❑ **How many feeling words do you know?**

Help your child expand his or her vocabulary or emotions with this activity. Have your child name an emotion, such as "bored," and then you give two or three related emotions (like lonely, weary, or restless). See if your child knows what these words mean, and if not, explain them. Describing emotions can be challenging, much like trying to describe a taste or color. It is often easier to define an emotion by describing a scenario to which your child can easily relate. Have your child name four to five emotions for you to supply similar but different feelings, and discuss how each emotion differs from similar emotions.

Grade 2

Resolving anger

❑ **What's really the problem?**

It is common for a child to display anger over something when the root of the problem lies elsewhere. Even adults do this! Successful resolution of anger depends on identifying the root cause. This activity can be done using imaginary scenarios when your child is feeling good ("How would you feel if...") or with an actual situation to which your child is reacting with anger. Help your child resolve the angry feelings by asking questions like, "What happened? Why did that happen? Why did that make you feel angry? Did something else about this situation make you mad? What led up to this situation?" Help your child talk through the issues to find the true cause of the anger and then work toward a solution.

Children often like to hear about when others had to deal with difficult situations, so feel free to share stories from your own life about times when you experienced strong emotions.

❑ **Problem solving**

There are times when we get mad at ourselves for something we've done or failed to do, or when something happens for which there is no one to blame. The next time your child expresses anger over something that happens, help him or her zero in on the problem and look for ways to fix it, if possible. For instance, if your child is angry because a fort he or she is building keeps falling apart, help your child pinpoint why this is happening. Brainstorm solutions by asking, "What can change this situation for the better?" Let your child try the various ideas until finding one that works, going from problem to accomplishment. This activity can introduce the importance of being kind to yourself and bring awareness to the fact that getting angry at yourself doesn't solve the problem. Making mistakes is part of living and learning, and it is often best to focus on how to correct mistakes rather than trying to ensure they never happen (impossible) or getting angry when they (inevitably) do.

❑ **Say it, stomp it, start over**

Here is an activity that gives your child a way to physically and verbally express anger, and then release it and move on. It has three parts:

1. Say it.
2. Stomp it.
3. Start over.

You can have your child practice this first for fun so that the next time anger bursts forth, your child will know what to do. First, have your child name the feeling and what has caused it (such as, "I am mad because there is no more milk and I want milk!"). Then have your child stomp around a bit, either making mad noises or using words ("No more milk! No more milk!"). After this has gone on for a minute or so, have your child take a deep breath and maybe shake out his or her arms and legs, and then start over with what he or she was doing before getting mad (in this case, getting a drink). The difference is that this time your child can approach the problem in a calmer way ("There's no more milk. What else can I drink?").

Grade 3
De-escalation techniques

❑ **Heading it off at the pass**

Learning to recognize emotional triggers allows you to avoid getting upset or to diffuse the situation before it can escalate. Ask your child to make a list of things that often bring on anger. For each item on the list, encourage your child to think about warning signs that signal the situation is about happen. Write these down. For instance, your child might get angry every time a younger sibling interrupts repeatedly when your child has a friend over to visit. The warning sign that anger might be triggered could be that there have already been two interruptions, or that the older two are involved in something that requires concentration, or that the younger child is tired or hungry (and thus more likely to need attention). Once the warning triggers are identified, help your child come up with a plan to use this awareness to prevent problems in the future.

- [ ] **Take a breath (or several)**

Many adults learn to take a few deep breaths to calm down when anger threatens. This simple technique can help you face a stressful situation in a more productive way. Children can be encouraged to use this technique, too. Teach your child to take a few deep breaths (or breathe deeply while counting to ten) and then try to view the situation in a calmer manner. You might also help your child think of activities that can help when life is stressful, such as deep breathing, going for a walk, spending time with a pet, or talking to a friend. You can share what works for you, and then your child can create a list of things to do to de-stress. This list can be added to over time.

- [ ] **Take a hike**

When two or more people are having trouble coming to an agreement or when emotions are making it difficult to work together, it can be very useful to take a break and do something physical together, such as a hike. This works for children and adults alike. The next time your child is feeling anger as a result of an interaction with someone else, try to take the two of them for a hike or a bike ride or a swim—anything that gets them in a new environment (preferably outdoors) and doing something they both enjoy. Chances are good that the problem will either dissolve and disappear, or the children will be able to come back to it with a new, productive mindset. Afterwards, make sure to discuss how and why this works.

Notes

Lesson

24 Unit IV Review: Self-Esteem

Place a checkmark by the activities that you have completed in this unit (lessons 19–23). Use this opportunity to review favorite topics or activities or try something new.

Lesson 19: Respect and Good Sportsmanship

KINDERGARTEN	**Respect for self and others** ❏ Golden rule ❏ Is it fair? ❏ Listening
GRADE 1	**Rules and fair play** ❏ Making the rules (and following them) ❏ You be the judge ❏ Equal vs. fair
GRADE 2	**Good sportsmanship** ❏ Win or lose with a smile ❏ Keeping score ❏ Beginner's luck
GRADE 3	**Dealing with disrespect** ❏ What would happen if...? ❏ Agree to disagree ❏ Stand up for your rights

Lesson 20: Social Skills

KINDERGARTEN	**Making friends** ❏ Friend card ❏ Friend pyramid ❏ It's your turn
GRADE 1	**Personal space** ❏ Space bubbles ❏ How small is your house? ❏ Too close, too far
GRADE 2	**Stand on your own two feet** ❏ Go your own way ❏ Marching to your own drummer ❏ Would you do what Simon says?
GRADE 3	**Dealing with bullying, teasing, and threats** ❏ Bad words, bad feelings ❏ Was that nice? ❏ Go wild

Lesson 21: Communication Skills

KINDERGARTEN	**Talking through problems** ❑ 1-2-3 Problem solving ❑ Striking a bargain ❑ Solutions instead of blame
GRADE 1	**Being a good listener** ❑ Do you hear what I hear? ❑ Find the word ❑ What did I say? What did I mean?
GRADE 2	**Self-advocacy (how to get what you need)** ❑ Strong vs. loud ❑ Asking instead of complaining ❑ What do I really want?
GRADE 3	**Nonverbal communication** ❑ Body talk ❑ Charades ❑ Model conversations

Lesson 22: Mentors and Elders

KINDERGARTEN	**Family and friends** ❑ Who do you love? ❑ Teach me how ❑ Family tree
GRADE 1	**Circle of support** ❑ From near to far ❑ Friends chain ❑ Rock-solid friends
GRADE 2	**Death is a part of life** ❑ Oldest person you know ❑ What to do when someone dies ❑ Feelings about death
GRADE 3	**Lending support to others** ❑ Who needs help? ❑ I'm good at... ❑ Good Deed Day

Lesson 23: Anger Management

KINDERGARTEN	**How to show your anger** ❑ Angry body ❑ Mad words, mean words ❑ Mad art
GRADE 1	**How do I really feel?** ❑ So many emotions ❑ That makes me feel... ❑ How many feeling words do you know?
GRADE 2	**Resolving anger** ❑ What's really the problem? ❑ Problem solving ❑ Say it, stomp it, start over
GRADE 3	**De-escalation techniques** ❑ Heading it off at the pass ❑ Take a breath (or several) ❑ Take a hike

Notes

Lesson

Challenges and Risks

Understanding how to handle both challenges and risks is part of growing up. Knowing your limits is as important as knowing when to push those limits. Recognizing how to gauge risk and accept challenges safely is the goal of these activities.

Kindergarten

Try and try again

❑ **What's easy? What's hard?**

Perseverance is not only an admirable quality, it is also an essential attribute of successful people. Ask your child to name three things that are easy to do and three things that are hard to do. Depending on your child, either list might include things like the following:

write the alphabet	pour a glass of milk
tie shoelaces	read a book
memorize phone numbers	play the piano
zip up a jacket	make toast

Tell your child that you will choose one action from the hard-to-do list that your child will try very hard to learn. Explain that sometimes we have to keep trying over and over without giving up, and this is what you'd like your child to do. Choose something that will be challenging for your child but do-able. Assist as needed, encouraging your child to stick with it until he or she succeeds. Afterward, congratulate your child heartily on all the hard work and sustained effort.

❑ **I have a dream**

Talk about a goal you have or one you have achieved and explain what you did, step by step, (or are doing) to make the goal a reality. Then ask your child to think of a goal or a dream that he or she would like to make come true. Keep talking about goals and dreams until one emerges that you think is achievable in the near future. This could be building a tree house, or creating an elaborate costume, or training a pet. Next, help your child list the steps needed to achieve this goal. Break down the steps into as many individual action items as you can in order to make it clear what, exactly, needs to be done to achieve the goal. Have your child check off items as they are completed so progress can be seen. Help your child follow through until the goal has been accomplished.

❏ **I bet I can**

In this challenging activity, you and your child will take turns pushing yourselves to new physical achievements. Focus on individual achievements, such as running faster than you did previously (rather than competitive achievements, such as running faster than someone else). Start each challenge with “I bet I can…” Here are a few ideas:

I bet I can…

- run to the mailbox before you can count to ten.
- jump over that cracked section of the pavement.
- leap up and touch the crooked branch on that tree.

The goal of this simple challenge is to encourage your child to push him- or herself to a greater accomplishment than might have been thought possible.

Grade 1

Handling failure and success

❏ **The ladder game**

Tell your child to imagine being a grown-up who has just accomplished a big goal. Name a goal that is related to your child’s interests: earning a spot in a ballet, winning an Olympic medal, learning to fly an airplane. Tell your child to imagine that this goal is the first rung on a ladder. What will this person do next? What is the next rung on the ladder? You might have your child draw a ladder to have a visual representation. Keep encouraging new ideas for each rung—help your child come up with related goals that are creative. For instance, the next step after learning to fly a plane might be flying a jet, and then flying a space shuttle, and then flying to Mars. The purpose of this exercise is to help your child view success as a process, not an end, so each success leads to a new goal.

❑ **Inventions gone awry**

Many, many inventions have been the result of a succession of failures. Visit the library or search online for stories about inventions and inventors, such as Ben Franklin, George Washington Carver, and Marie Curie. Talk about what would have happened if these inventors had given up with the first failed experiment.

❑ **Super powers**

Ask your child to imagine what it would be like to never fail. What if you never fell or hurt yourself or made a mistake? What if you never had your feelings hurt? What if you never failed at anything you tried to do? What would you be like as a friend? What kind of parent would a "super person" like this be? At first, your child may only see this in terms of positive outcomes: being able to do anything, able to help others, able to take risks without worry. You may want to add your own thoughts about what it would be like to be invincible, or what it would be like to know someone like that, possibly injecting a bit of reality into this fantasy situation by pointing out that this person might be hard to keep up with, or might have unrealistic expectations of others or feelings of superiority. You may want to help your child consider how mistakes and failures lead to a more resilient human being, or how our experiences (both good and bad) can make us more compassionate, patient, and wise.

Grade 2
Challenging yourself

❑ **Think big**

Ask your child to name several things he or she does well or particularly enjoys doing. Then daydream together about where these interests and abilities might eventually lead. Encourage your child to dream big! Have your child draw an illustration of one (or several) of these big dreams.

❑ **With one hand behind my back**

Are you familiar with the saying, "I can do that with one hand tied behind my back"? This is a jaunty way to express complete confidence in your abilities. In this challenging activity, your child will try, with one hand behind the back, to do ordinary things at which he or she is quite good. This challenge requires perseverance and creative problem solving, and may give your child a new confidence in his or her ability to tackle a good challenge.

❑ **Champion athletes**

Does your family enjoy watching sports on TV or attending sports events? Does your child have an interest in a particular sport? In this activity, you and your child will learn about someone who is a sports champion. Find out all you can about this inspiring person, including the obstacles he or she had to overcome and the difficult challenges that were faced on the way to success.

Grade 3

Risk taking and understanding your limits

❑ **Is the risk worth the reward?**

Weighing the risk of an activity against the possible reward is a complex and sophisticated skill. This activity will help your child begin to understand the process. You and your child are going to consider several types of challenges that involve serious risks. If you can, find some photos of these activities to help your child envision the scenario more fully. Choose a few from the list below or come up with your own:

- climbing Mt. Everest
- living on the International Space Station

- backpacking in the wilderness
- sky diving
- scuba diving
- sailing solo across the ocean
- swimming the English Channel

Then, pose the following questions:

1. What are the risks?
2. What are the rewards?
3. Do you think the risk is worth the reward?

You may not know all the answers to these questions but just discussing the possibilities will help your child begin to develop the tools for risk assessment.

❑ **Drawing the line**

In this activity, you are going to encourage your child to consider his or her willingness to participate in various challenging activities. Begin by having your child choose one of the challenging activities from the list in the previous exercise. Draw a line on paper (like a number line) and put that behavior on the far right end of your line. Write down a few related activities of varying intensity along the line, and on the far left write, "Not willing to do this at all." For instance, a line for climbing Mt. Everest might have benchmarks for climbing Denali, climbing a local mountain, hiking a steep hill, and hiking a flat trail.

Once several degrees of participation are in place, ask your child to draw a colored line across the activity line at the point where he or she would be willing to participate. Next, have your child draw another colored line showing what he or she might wish to be able to do in one year, and another line for five years from now. These three lines might all be in the same place, or your child may display a willingness to tackle greater challenges in the coming years. This can open a discussion about the importance of being realistic about your abilities, and about how what you are willing and able to do is likely to change over time. If you'd like, you can describe an experience from your life that illustrates this.

❑ **Paying the price**

Spinal cord injuries and brain injuries are serious, life-altering consequences that sometimes follow risky behaviors. These injuries can occur from riding a bike or motorcycle without a helmet, riding in a car without a seatbelt, diving headfirst into shallow water, or falling from a substantial height. Of course, many injuries are from accidents in which the injured person did nothing risky or neglectful—we wouldn't want to make any assumptions about a person based on his or her injury. However, it may be useful for your child to learn a little about what can happen in the body when there is a spinal cord injury or a brain injury. Library books and online research can also reveal advances in medical treatment and mobility options for people with these injuries.

Lesson

Decision Making

It can be difficult to make a decision and even harder to accept the consequences of that decision. Children often find themselves regretting a simple decision ("I wanted the vanilla, not the chocolate!"). This lesson helps children explore the many facets of the decision-making process.

Kindergarten
Choices

❑ **You choose**

Adults make decisions, big and small, all day long. What shall I eat for breakfast? In what order will I do the errands and chores today? Should I homeschool my children or send them to school? If I choose school, what school would be best for them? Over the next week, tell your child that he or she will be in charge of some of these daily decisions (the small ones, naturally). Make sure to choose ones for which your child's decision will be fine, or narrow the choices to make it more practical. Instead of asking, "What shall we eat for dinner?", you might ask "Shall we have pesto pasta for dinner or tacos?" Allowing your child the opportunity to make these decisions gives him or her a sense of the freedom and responsibility of decision making.

❑ **Would you rather...?**

In this game, you'll ask a series of hypothetical questions that present your child with two choices. These questions can be about food, activities, music, or anything else you can think of (a few ideas are below). It doesn't matter if your child doesn't yet have direct experience with some of the options. The goal is to allow your child the experience of making a choice. If you'd like, you can discuss how he or she arrived at the decision, and thus begin to bring attention to the decision-making process.

Would you rather...

- eat watermelon or cheese?
- ride a bike or ride a horse?
- go to the beach or go to the mountains?
- live in a small house with a big yard or a big house with a small yard?
- listen to music or play a musical instrument?
- have a dog or a cat for a pet?

❑ **Eeny, meeny, miney, moe**

There are times when a decision is hard to make because both options are agreeable or equally desirable. Many people—adults included—resort to a random choice at times like this: a coin toss, a blind choice (choose what's in someone's right or left hand), or a childhood chant that eliminates the possibilities until only one is left. If you know a chant (like eeny, meeny, miney, moe), teach it to your child and encourage him or her to use it the next time a tough decision arrives. Sometimes it is only by eliminating possibilities that we realize what it is that we truly want. If your child makes a final decision that is different than what the random choice indicated, that works, too. Techniques that narrow down the choices are all part of the process of defining the best option.

Grade 1
Sticking with your decision and changing your mind

❑ **Guess the consequences**

In this activity, you'll be creating a town with your child, drawing it on paper very simply. There are many, many decisions to be made:

- Where will the roads go?
- Is there a river or lake in or near your town?
- Where will the houses go?
- Will there be a park or bike paths?
- What businesses will your town have?

- What will your town be called?

As your child makes these decisions, bring up the possible consequences of the choices, both good and bad. If you don't have a river, it might be hard to find a source of fresh water; if you do have a river, there are certain businesses that could benefit from being close to it. If the grocery story is close to the houses, people can walk there. But if the houses are set apart from the businesses, they can have bigger yards. Will the park be downtown, in the neighborhoods, or in a more rural part? What are the pros and cons of each of these options? Discuss decisions and consequences in relation to one another ("If we do this, then that will happen."). Have your child continue to draw, enhance, and embellish the town as new ideas come to light.

❑ **Now that I think about it...**

It often happens in daily life that a decision or opinion we hold gets reconsidered when we learn new information. The next time this happens, discuss it with your child, pointing out your initial reasoning, and how the new information changed your thinking. Let your child know that it is okay to change your mind. For instance, you might have been planning to make lasagna for dinner, but when you realized you didn't have all the ingredients, you changed your mind and decided on something else. Or perhaps your friends were coming for the weekend and you planned a day hike but then it rained and you had to change plans. Or it could be something more significant: you were planning to buy a certain car, but after checking its safety rating, you decided on another model. Be on the lookout for when your child has the opportunity to reconsider a decision, and discuss the process of making a decision and then reviewing it in light of new developments.

❑ **Living with your decision**

The next time you go food shopping, you can do this activity, which lets your child experience what it is like to make a choice that can't be changed. Allow your child to choose one or more food items to buy. For instance, if you are buying cereal, let your child choose which one (among several acceptable options), or if you need pasta sauce, let your child make the choice. Explain that food can't be returned once it's been opened and tasted so whatever item is chosen, the whole family will have to eat it. Hopefully, the chosen food item will be delicious, but if not, encourage your child to eat it anyway, while keeping in mind that the next time, he or she can choose something else that will be more satisfactory.

Grade 2

Who gets to decide?

❑ Who is in control?

There are many decisions in life that are in our control and many that are not. Your child may or may not be aware that even parents are not in charge of everything that gets decided. Use the following list (and add to it) and ask your child to guess who has the power to decide in each situation:

- when bedtime is
- traffic laws
- what to buy at the store
- what game to play
- spelling rules
- what clothes to wear
- which friends are invited over
- whether or not to wear a jacket outside
- what book to read
- what movie to see
- who gets to be president
- what music is listened to in the car

❑ Making decisions for the group

Sometimes a group of people make a decision collectively, and other times one person (a teacher, parent, or boss, for instance) makes a decision that will affect the entire group. There is a responsibility in making a decision on behalf of others. Discuss with your child some of the issues to consider, such as the health and welfare of the group, the desires or opinions of individual members of the group, and the overall purpose or goal of the group. Give specific examples from your own life, if possible. Look for an opportunity for your child to be responsible for making a decision for the whole group. For instance, if your extended family is gathering, perhaps your child could decide on an activity the whole group could do together. Help your child consider the relevant aspects before making a final choice.

- [ ] **Group decision making**

The group decision-making process can be complex and lengthy, but to introduce your child to the concept, you can present it with the following simple steps.

1. Explore the options.
2. Get everyone's input.
3. Discuss the pros and cons of each option.
4. Narrow down the options, if possible.
5. Cast votes.
6. Use majority rule, or, if ruling by consensus, continue with steps 1–5 until a unanimous decision is reached.

If possible, engage in this process the next time a group of people (of which your child is part) is making a decision. It can be something simple, like choosing a movie to watch or a restaurant to visit, or something more significant, such as the destination for a family vacation.

Grade 3

Making good decisions

❏ **Big 3**

Good decisions don't just happen by chance (not usually, anyway). They are the result of using reason and good judgment to determine which choice will lead to the best outcome. When children become teens, they are often faced with increasingly important decisions. Introducing your child to these three simple questions now will help him or her incorporate them into the decision-making process before the consequences of a poor decision become great.

1. Is it safe?
2. Is it legal?
3. Would you want your family to know?

Discuss how to use these as a measuring stick, and why each is important. Depending on your child and your situation, you may want to use these questions to discuss alcohol, tobacco, and drug use, abuse, and prevention.

❏ **Will it matter?**

Often the decisions we make that seem so urgent and important at the time are forgotten or rendered insignificant in a very short period of time. When your child faces what seems like a huge dilemma, advise him or her to consider these questions:

- Will what I choose matter one hour from now?
- Will it matter in one day?
- Will it matter in one week?
- Will it matter in one year?

This simple technique gives your child a tool to put things into perspective. If possible, find a real life example to illustrate this.

❑ **Seven generations**

Are you familiar with the Native American concept of looking seven generations into the future to weigh the possible consequences of an action? You can introduce this thoughtful, forward-thinking idea to your child with this activity. Have your child plant an acorn or some other (local) tree seed in your yard, or in the woods nearby. As it is being planted, daydream with your child about all the fun ways the tree might be used as it grows—for a rope swing, climbing, a tree house, gathering nuts and leaves—and about all the things the tree might see in its lifetime. Then have your child figure out how many years it would have to grow in order to still be around for children to play beneath it seven generations ahead. (Figure each generation is about 25 years and have your child do the math.) Try to imagine what the tree will see in seven generations, and what the land around it will look like by then.

Notes

Lesson 27 Public Safety

Laws, local regulations, and common customs are designed to maintain a safe environment for the community, but public safety also depends on the actions of individuals. The activities in this lesson highlight ways each person can contribute to creating a safe, healthy place to live.

Kindergarten
Crosswalks and traffic signs

❏ **Reading signs and symbols**

Learning to understand the many traffic signs and symbols is something even pre-readers can do. While you are traveling around town, take the time to point out signs and explain their meanings. (Alternately, you can get a picture book from the library about signs and symbols.) After seeing a particular sign several times, ask your child, "What does that mean?" Be on the lookout for signs like these:

stop
crosswalk
railroad crossing
bike path
hospital
yield

stoplight ahead
no parking
workers ahead
slippery when wet
falling rock
deer crossing

❏ **Hand signals**

Even if your child doesn't yet ride a bike, hand signals are good to know (and fun to use). Find a place outdoors where you can pretend to be driving cars or riding bikes, and play Follow the Leader. Maneuver along an imaginary route that is full of turns and stops. Use hand signals to warn the person behind you of what you are doing next: left arm held out to the left for a left turn; left arm bent at the elbow, hand pointing up, for a right turn; and left arm held down to the side for slow down or stop. Take turns being the leader and using the hand signals to indicate your actions.

❑ **Traffic lights**

Intersections are an excellent place to watch traffic lights and become familiar with their green-yellow-red pattern. Find an intersection with a traffic light and cross walks. Let your child push the crosswalk button, and then watch the traffic light change from green to yellow to red before you can cross the street. Walk to the next corner, and let your child push the crosswalk button to cross the connecting street (you will eventually work your way around all four sides of the intersection). As your child becomes cued in to the pattern of the traffic lights, ask him or her to predict which color will appear next. This is also a great opportunity to discuss crosswalk safety, such as staying within the lines of the crosswalk, walking briskly while crossing, waiting for the signal, etc.

Grade 1

Public gatherings

❑ **Meeting spot**

When two or more people want to meet, they arrange a meeting spot. Likewise, when a group of people splits up to pursue their own interests but want to regroup later, they choose a meeting spot. Familiarize your child with this idea—it may come in handy in the future if you ever get split up and need to find one another again. Go to a park or an open space, and help your child choose a good place to meet. Choose a place that is central, easy to find, and easy to spot from a distance. Next, arrange with your child to meet at this spot in one minute, and then wander off in opposite directions. (Of course, you'll want to make sure you are in a safe place for this.) In one minute, make your way to the meeting spot. Hopefully your child will have gotten there first. Choose a different meeting spot and repeat. When you are in town or at a large gathering, make a point of identifying a good meeting place in case anyone gets separated.

❑ **Public restrooms**

Many families have specific rules for public restrooms, and children need to be taught these rules, which are often very different from the rules for the home bathroom. If you are visiting the library, a restaurant, or a store this week, visit the public restroom and talk about the health and safety rules. Depending on your child and your situation, you may want to explain why these rules are important, or just give a general explanation, such as, "Since so many people use this restroom, we want to make sure we're careful about germs."

❑ **Be sense-able**

Being aware of one's surroundings is an important part of being safe in public places. In this activity, you'll use your senses to pick up clues about your environment. This works best in a busy place like a mall, fair, or city street. Walk until you smell a distinctive, familiar smell. This may be a pizza place, candle shop, hot dog stand, shoe store, perfume counter, Chinese restaurant, fish market, street repairs truck, or anything with a distinctive smell. Stop and ask your child to close his or her eyes and try to identify or describe the smell. Continue walking and stopping to try to identify different smells.

Grade 2
Sharing resources

❑ **Leave only footprints**

Sharing resources, like our state parks, carries with it the inherent responsibility to help care for the resource and make it last. Take a trip to a state or national park nearby. As you hike, look for a place to make footprints: a dusty path, a muddy stream bank, or a dirt clearing. Spend a few minutes making foot prints to leave behind. You can do this randomly, or make a kind of family footprint picture in the dirt. Continue with your hike as you explain that those footprints are the only things you'll leave behind when you exit the park. All your trash and belongings will be taken with you, and you'll leave trails, plants, and animals as undisturbed as possible.

❑ **Water ways**

What are the ways in which we care for water that is shared by the public? Drinking fountains, water features (fish ponds, fountains, waterfalls), public swimming pools, ponds, and streams—water is all around us. It's important to respect and protect the cleanliness and beauty of this water for the enjoyment and health of all. Visit as many water sites as you can, discussing the different (often unspoken) rules for each. Here are a few things you might mention.

- Drinking fountains: don't put your mouth on anything but the water; it is okay to fill up your water bottle; get a drink and step aside quickly if others are waiting.
- Water features (fish ponds, fountains, waterfalls): Toss in a penny and make a wish; don't fish out the money you see; don't throw anything else in (food, trash, spit, etc.).
- Public swimming pools: Use the bathroom before you get in the pool (don't pee in the pool); follow the safety rules; obey the lifeguard.
- Ponds and streams: don't throw in anything (pennies, trash); don't disturb the wildlife or plants; some streams are okay to dam but remove the dam before you leave; don't drink the water unless you boil it or purify it first.

❑ **Everyone's Earth**

Ask your child to write a list of all the ways in which people can care for the Earth. You may have to help by suggesting ideas, or your child may be very aware of Earth stewardship. Encourage your child to make this list into an illustrated or decorated sign to post at home to help remind everyone of the many things they can do to help the Earth. Here are a few ideas:

- recycle
- plant a garden
- compost kitchen scraps
- conserve water
- turn off lights when not in use
- hang clothes outside to dry

Grade 3

Doing your part to keep the public safe

Every little bit helps

No one likes to see litter, but sometimes we are the unknowing cause of it: a scrap of paper falls out of the car door or window, a piece of plastic blows away as bags are being carried, or an aluminum can bounces out of the back of a pickup on the way to the recycling center. Take a walk in your neighborhood, along a beach or creek, or in a park, and bring along a bag to collect litter and dispose of it. Have your child help pick up litter, or (if cleanliness is a concern) have your child hold the bag while you do the clean-up. Discuss the many ways litter occurs, and brainstorm how it might be prevented.

Part of the plan

Every public place has rules, whether they are posted or not. Visit an outdoor public space, such as a playground, park, trail, or open space. Look for signs and discuss the purpose behind each posted rule. In the absence of signs, talk about general rules (and the purpose behind them):

- Stay on the trail.
- Open from sunrise to sunset.
- No camping.
- No alcohol or glass containers.
- No open fires.
- Do not feed the wildlife.

What did you see?

Find a place outdoors in nature, preferably a place with which you and your child are not familiar. Explain that you will both have 30 seconds to take in your surroundings, and then 30 seconds to picture it in your mind's eyes (with eyes closed) before writing down ten specific things that you noticed. Use a watch and time yourselves. Observe for 30 seconds, turning around to take in as much as possible. Reflect silently for 30 seconds, with eyes closed. Finally, make your lists, without conferring or looking around. Be very descriptive and specific. Rather than listing, "a tree, a boulder, a bird," write down, "a tree with a broken branch on the left side halfway up, a boulder shaped like a whale, a bird with a yellow spot on the wing and a long beak." Compare notes and see how much each of you was able to recall. If that seemed too easy, choose another spot and try to recall 25 things after 15 seconds of observation and 15 seconds of reflection. Paying attention to the beauty around us in nature can help us develop a greater appreciation for it and a heightened sense of stewardship.

Lesson 28 Emergency Situations

While most children will never find themselves in an emergency situation without adult help, preparation and knowledge can help them stay safe. When choosing scenarios to work with in these activities, make sure to choose ones you are comfortable with. It can be frightening to consider various emergency situations and children and adults alike can become anxious when discussing emergencies. The goal of this lesson is to empower your child with knowledge, not to worry him or her with alarming possibilities. You know your child best and can adapt these activities to provide a supportive and helpful lesson.

Kindergarten
Who can help?

❑ **Helpers everywhere**

While you are out and about this week, make a point of noticing all the different people and organizations you notice whose job is to help in an emergency situation. You might see police (or police cars and police station), firefighters (or trucks and station), hospital workers, ambulance and EMTs, Red Cross, National Guard, or other military personnel. You might expand your circle of helpers to include school crossing guards, teachers, city bus drivers, park rangers, city maintenance workers, and your neighbors, depending on your situation.

❑ **What to do when you need help**

Asking for help can be hard for children, so it's a good idea to practice. You can begin by pretending you need to ask for help together, and making up different situations where you might need to call for help or ask someone you see. If your child is willing, you can role play to make this fun and present scenarios that will be helpful to your child (and not scary). Here's a simple scenario you might want to begin with: You can pretend to be the neighbor and your child is going to ask you for help because Mom is feeling sick. Next, you might pretend to be a police officer and your child is lost and needs to ask for help, or you can pretend to be a firefighter who is coming to put out a fire at your house and your child needs to ask for help in rescuing the dog or cat. The goal is to have your child get used to the idea that when there is an emergency situation of any kind, there are lots of people who can help.

If your child hasn't already learned his or her address and phone number, you can find a familiar tune (like "Twinkle, Twinkle Little Star") and put your information to the tune to make it easier to remember. You can also have your child practice using the phone to call home or call a parent's cell phone, and talk about when and why to call 911.

❑ **Staying safe in scary situations**

Earthquakes, fires, floods, blizzards, and hurricanes are all examples of scary emergency situations that your child might experience. Depending on where you live, have a conversation about some of the emergency situations your child might encounter. Focus on how to stay safe in an emergency situation. Is there a place in your house where you go during a hurricane or earthquake? Does your child know not to hide when something scary happens, but to seek an adult or call for help? Talk about how your family prepares for emergencies and what your child can do to help.

Grade 1
Fire safety

❑ **Safety rules**

Fire safety rules can be found in many sources online or at your local firehouse. Talk about the rules with your child, and practice them. Here are some important rules (you might find or think of more):

- Don't play with matches or lighters.
- If you smell or see fire, go and tell someone.
- If there is smoke in the house, get down on the floor and crawl to safety.
- Never hide in a closet or under a bed when there is a fire.
- If your clothes catch on fire, stop, drop, and roll to put out the fire.

- If there is a fire, don't go back into the house once you leave—let the firefighters do that.

❑ **Visit to the firehouse**

Visiting the firehouse is always very exciting with its big trucks, intriguing gear and equipment, and friendly firefighters. To prepare in advance, you can find library books to read or come up with a list of questions to ask. Call the firehouse before you visit to ask if you need to make an appointment.

❑ **Making a fire and putting it out**

Making and tending a fire (and safely putting it out) are practical skills. First, teach your child how to safely light a match or lighter, and have him or her practice lighting a candle, and then putting it out. Next, demonstrate fire building and tending. Allow your child to do as much of the work as possible. Talk about how to keep safe while starting and tending a fire. If you don't have a fire pit, you can build a fire in a large sandbox, or dig a shallow hole in the ground and line it with rocks. Have your child help collect kindling and sticks, making piles of all the different sizes needed to build a good fire. You might want to cook over your fire (shish kebabs, hot dogs, and marshmallows are favorite fire-cooked foods) before you safely put it out with dirt, water, or sand.

Grade 2
Electricity and lightning

❑ Storm safety

If you are caught outside in a lightning storm, do you know what to do? Here are some safety tips to talk about and practice with your child.

- If you can reach a large building, take shelter inside. A large, enclosed building is the best shelter. Once inside, stay a few feet away from windows, electrical boxes, and outlets.
- You can take shelter in a hard-topped car as well. Roll the windows up and don't touch anything metal.
- If you are outside and can't reach shelter, find a low place away from tall trees, anything metal (such as fences, culverts, or sheds), or anything tall. Crouch down to make yourself smaller.
- If you are on or in the water when thunder starts, get out of the water immediately and find shelter.
- If you feel a tingling sensation, lightning may be very near. Crouch down on the balls of your feet, lower your head, and place your hands over your ears. Get as low as possible without putting your hands or knees on the ground. Do not lie down.

❑ Learn about lightning

There are some amazing videos online about how lightning occurs, including slow motion videos that show the path of lightning (from clouds to ground, from ground to clouds, and between clouds). Visit the library and search online for remarkable facts, important safety information, and astonishing videos of lightning.

❑ Shelter in a storm

In this activity, your child can point out places in the environment (wherever you happen to be at the time) that are safe to shelter in during a storm. Try to do this in several different places, such as your neighborhood, the town, a park, etc. Remember that a large enclosed building is safe in a lightning storm, but a small shelter or open pavilion may not be. Talk to your child about being aware of the weather when a storm is developing and finding shelter before the storm hits, if possible.

Grade 3

When to get help

- ❑ **Is this an emergency?**

It can be helpful to have a conversation about what is truly an emergency and what is simply something that feels urgent (but doesn't include the risk of bodily injury or property damage). Ask your child to name a few emergency situations, such as an uncontrolled fire or a flood. You might add a few to the list, and then begin naming a situation and asking your child, "Is this an emergency?" For instance, you might ask, "The car gets a flat tire while we're driving on the freeway. Is this an emergency?" or "You swallow a mouthful of water while you are swimming with friends. Is this an emergency?" This can lead into a discussion about how something can turn into an emergency quickly (a mouthful of water can lead to choking and near-drowning), or how quick thinking can keep something from becoming an emergency (grabbing a nearby plastic raft can keep you afloat while you get your breath back).

- ❑ **Calling 911**

While young children may not have the ability to judge when a 911 emergency call is warranted, your third grader is probably able to understand that 911 calls are only made in serious emergencies. In order to help your child feel prepared and capable, you can practice placing an emergency call. Unplug or turn off the phone before you begin. You can also have your child practice without a phone, but holding and speaking into a phone (one that's turned off) will help make the situation more realistic. You can pretend to be the 911 operator, and ask the following types of questions: "911 operator, what is your emergency? Where are you? What is your name? Don't hang up, help is on the way." Coach your child on how to answer, based on several different emergency scenarios.

❑ **Helping the helpers**

When help arrives in an emergency situation, children are often frightened and afraid to speak. Talk about ways to help in an emergency situation. Here are some ideas, and you can add ideas of your own.

- Don't hide when firefighters, police, or paramedics arrive.
- Tell them who you are and where you live.
- Explain what happened or describe what you saw.
- Stay where you are unless someone in charge tells you to move.

Lesson 29 Technology, Media, and Health

Using technology means using our bodies to interact with a machine. Even ergonomic computers and personal devices can place stress on the human body. In addition, active motion tends to decrease in direct proportion to an increase in screen time. An overemphasis on sedentary pursuits (such as sitting in front of a screen) puts undue stress on the physical body, especially a growing one—active play is essential to a healthy childhood. Addressing the many health issues related to technology and media is the topic of this lesson.

Kindergarten
What is screen time?

❑ **Count the screens**

While parents often struggle to limit screen time and media influence, children are often unaware of what constitutes screen time. This simple exercise can help them become aware of the many electronic devices in their lives. Becoming aware of how often screens are used is the first step toward monitoring and/or limiting screen time. Ask your child to go through the entire house and count the number of electronic screens. This may include TVs, computer monitors, laptops, cell phones, iPads, Kindles, etc. Next, have your child count the number of screens he or she looks at regularly. Talk about any family rules you may have for limiting or monitoring screen time, and the reasoning behind these rules.

❑ **Stretch breaks**

In order to help underscore how your body feels after sitting for a long while (for example, during the length of an average children's movie or television program), encourage stretch breaks anytime your child is doing a screen-based activity for longer than fifteen minutes. Set a timer for fifteen minutes, and when it goes off, have your child do one minute of simple stretching exercises (you can keep the movie going or pause it, whichever works best). Set the timer for another fifteen minutes and then do another minute of stretching. Repeat throughout the length of the program. Your child may feel a little annoyed at having the program interrupted but the stretching will probably feel very good and any initial resistance may go away.

❑ **Be kind to eyes**

We ask our eyes to work very hard during the day, no matter what we do. These simple eye care activities give busy eyes a chance to rest. Teach these two techniques to your child, and use them yourself frequently to demonstrate how easy it is to incorporate them into the day.

1. Palming: Cup your hands over closed eyes (don't press on the eyelids). Right away you'll probably feel the warmth of your palms warming and relaxing the little muscles around your eyes. Count to ten slowly.
2. Outlining: With eyes closed, gently use your fingertips to trace the outline of your eyebrows (both at the same time) and then along the ridge of bone under your eyes. Trace these lines, above and below the eyes, a few times, gently massaging the muscles around the eyes.

Grade 1

Media influence on health choices

❑ **Cereal box beauty contest**

To demonstrate how advertising affects health choices, take your child to the grocery store when you have some extra time. Stand in the cereal aisle and have your child point to a few different boxes that are attention grabbing. Discuss what makes them appealing, and then discuss the nutritional content of what's inside. Find a few nutritional products and compare the design of the packaging. Is the oatmeal package focusing on its nutrition while the sugary cereal package focuses on fun or media tie-ins? Does the sweetened cereal packaging promote its health benefits while downplaying the high sugar/calorie content? Talk about how big companies often have teams of people working to create advertising and packaging design that appeal to children and/or adults so that they will choose that product, regardless of its nutritional content.

❑ **Happy eaters**

If you watch TV in your home or have magazines featuring candy or snack foods, this activity is a good way to focus your child's awareness on how these ads equate happiness with eating these types of snacks. Find several ads and talk about how those eating the snack foods are portrayed. Do the models in the ads look happy? Active? Healthy and fit? Explain how people who regularly purchase and consume these foods may not be either active or healthy, and how the ad gives a false impression of what will happen if you eat this product.

❑ **What is it trying to get me to do?**

Every ad has a purpose in mind: to sell more products. Sometimes this is done by creating a desire, sometimes by encouraging overconsumption, sometimes by implying an added benefit (such as a happier life, more friends, better job, etc.). Sit down with your child and look at a few ads (print or TV) and ask your child to try to figure out what the ad is trying to accomplish. Ask questions to help your child see beyond the surface: Does this ad want to you be active? Does it want you to eat something? Is it trying to convince you to buy more than you normally would need or want?

Grade 2
Vision, posture, and hearing

❑ **Ergonomics (making your work space fit your body)**

Many adults are careful to customize their work spaces to be ergonomically correct because they know from experience how easily injuries can occur from poorly aligned or designed spaces: repetitive stress injuries, back problems, stiff neck and shoulders, vision difficulties, etc. Children are just as much in need of ergonomically designed work spaces when they begin to sit for long periods of time. However, children in the younger grades often move around frequently when working, work for shorter periods of time, and have many places in which they regularly do work: the dining room table, the couch, the kitchen counter, the car, the floor, etc. Choose one or more places where your child often sits to work, and consider the ergonomics of the work space, based on the following principles. When your child is ready for a more permanent work space, these principles can help you create a healthy, productive, and ergonomically correct area.

- Chair: Can your feet rest flat on the floor? Does your chair support your back in an upright position or does it encourage slumping? Are your thighs roughly parallel to the floor? Is your chair aligned with your workspace so that both your focal point (book, paper, or computer monitor) and your hands (keyboard or paper) are directly in front of your body?
- Desk: Do you have enough room for the things you need to have near you while you work? Are your hands, when resting on the desk, paper, or keyboard, a comfortable distance from your body (not too close, not too far)? When writing or typing, is your wrist slightly lower than your elbow?
- Vision: If using a monitor, is it a comfortable distance away to enable you to see it clearly? Do you have to look up, down, or to the side in order to see the screen easily? When you are reading or using the computer, do you take regular eye breaks? The suggested 20/20/20 rule is to look away from your work for 20 seconds every 20 minutes and focus on something at least 20 feet away. Practice this so you have an idea of a good place to look during your regular eye breaks.

❏ **Ear test**

While many teens use ear buds for hours at a time, this is not usually an issue for younger children. However, this exercise can give your child a clear picture of the issues with ear bud use so that if and when the time comes, he or she will have prior knowledge of how to avoid problems. This can be done either using ear buds or by turning the volume up loud on music, a movie, or a video game. First, have a whispered conversation when it is quiet. See how many small sounds you can hear, indoors or out. In quiet voices, draw each other's attention to everything you can hear. Next, spend five minutes listening to something at a very loud volume—obviously, you don't want the volume so loud that it hurts, but turn it up as loud as you might at a party or when there is a big group in the room. Alternately, you can mow the lawn or use another loud machine with your child nearby. After five minutes, turn it off, and repeat your whispered conversation, trying very hard to hear all the little things you heard before. Has your ability to hear quiet sounds diminished temporarily? Can you hear a whisper as easily? Talk about how hearing often gets temporarily affected but that permanent damage can occur after prolonged exposure to loud sounds.

- **Create your own space**

Using the principles of ergonomics listed in the activity above, help your child create a work area (desk and chair) that fits his or her body. Depending on the furniture you have available, this might require some ingenious adaptations. For instance, a crate with a firm pillow cushion might be just the right seat height, or perhaps an end table can be converted into a child-sized desk. You may not be able to create a work space that is practical for permanent use (you might need that crate or end table for something else or your child might outgrow them rather quickly), but the process of creating a work area that is fitted to your child's size and shape will provide an important framework for the future.

Grade 3

The picture of health (beauty in advertising)

- **Who looks like that?**

Advertising tends to promote an unrealistic view of style, beauty, wealth, and opportunity. Using ads you see in magazines, on billboards, and in TV promotions, have your child compare what the ads portray with what he or she has seen or experienced in daily life. Do the houses look like anyone's house you know? Do the models dress like people you know? Are the models doing ordinary things (such as shopping or cooking) in beautiful clothes with carefully arranged hair and makeup? Does anyone you know look like that when they are shopping or cooking? Depending on your child and your views, you may want to continue the conversation into the topic of how ads portray women, or how they can affect the self-esteem of viewers who are not wealthy or beautiful, or how beauty in advertising is often equated with health and happiness, but, in reality, the opposite is frequently the case.

- **Health in all shapes and sizes**

Real life athletes—both professionals and ordinary, everyday fitness enthusiasts—provide a welcome alternative to the image of beauty often portrayed in the media. Find photos online or in fitness and health magazines, or spend some time in a place where runners, swimmers, bicyclists, or other fitness enthusiasts are likely to be (the gym, park, or bike path are great places). Talk about how fitness affects health (and, if you'd like, how health affects overall attractiveness), and how people of all shapes and sizes can be healthy and fit. Compare the fairly narrow view of beauty and health portrayed in advertisements (usually people who are tall and slim, with carefully groomed hair and clothing, and no blemishes or distinguishing marks) with the wide variety of body types you see in the real world, among people with active lifestyles.

❑ **Tricks of the trade**

At times, it can be difficult to figure out what an ad is selling, even if you read the fine print. Whenever you see an ad, ask your child, "What do you think they are trying to sell in this ad?" Once your child makes a guess, you can reveal the real purpose of the ad (if you can figure it out!). Discuss how advertisers often use appealing images (such as a puppy or a beautifully dressed woman) to draw in a viewer's attention, and then give their message with a few subtle words or even just a logo or subtle product placement (a very carefully revealed expensive wristwatch on a well-dressed man driving a luxury car, for instance).

Lesson

30 Unit V Review: Self and Community

Check off the activities that have been completed in unit five (lessons 25–29). Spend some time reviewing material you covered in this unit. Explore new activities or related topics, as desired.

Lesson 25: Challenges and Risks

KINDERGARTEN	**Try and try again** ❑ What's easy? What's hard? ❑ I have a dream ❑ I bet I can
GRADE 1	**Handling failure and success** ❑ The ladder game ❑ Inventions gone awry ❑ Super powers
GRADE 2	**Challenging yourself** ❑ Think big ❑ With one hand behind my back ❑ Champion athletes
GRADE 3	**Risk taking and understanding your limits** ❑ Is the risk worth the reward? ❑ Drawing the line ❑ Paying the price

Lesson 26: Decision Making

KINDERGARTEN	**Choices** ❏ You choose ❏ Would you rather...? ❏ Eeny, meeny, miney, moe
GRADE 1	**Sticking with your decision and changing your mind** ❏ Guess the consequences ❏ Now that I think about it... ❏ Living with your decision
GRADE 2	**Who gets to decide?** ❏ Who is in control? ❏ Making decisions for the group ❏ Group decision making
GRADE 3	**Making good decisions** ❏ Big 3 ❏ Will it matter? ❏ Seven generations

Lesson 27: Public Safety

KINDERGARTEN	**Crosswalks and traffic signs** ❑ Reading signs and symbols ❑ Hand signals ❑ Traffic lights
GRADE 1	**Public gatherings** ❑ Meeting spot ❑ Public restrooms ❑ Be sense-able
GRADE 2	**Sharing resources** ❑ Leave only footprints ❑ Water ways ❑ Everyone's Earth
GRADE 3	**Doing your part to keep the public safe** ❑ Every little bit helps ❑ Part of the plan ❑ What did you see?

Lesson 28: Emergency Situations

KINDERGARTEN	**Who can help?** ❑ Helpers everywhere ❑ What to do when you need help ❑ Staying safe in scary situations
GRADE 1	**Fire safety** ❑ Safety rules ❑ Visit to the firehouse ❑ Making a fire and putting it out
GRADE 2	**Electricity and lightning** ❑ Storm safety ❑ Learn about lightning ❑ Shelter in a storm
GRADE 3	**When to get help** ❑ Is this an emergency? ❑ Calling 911 ❑ Helping the helpers

Lesson 29: Technology, Media, and Health

KINDERGARTEN	**What is screen time?** ❑ Count the screens ❑ Stretch breaks ❑ Be kind to eyes
GRADE 1	**Media influence on health choices** ❑ Cereal box beauty contest ❑ Happy eaters ❑ What is it trying to get me to do?
GRADE 2	**Vision, posture, and hearing** ❑ Ergonomics (making your work space fit your body) ❑ Ear test ❑ Create your own space
GRADE 3	**The picture of health (beauty in advertising)** ❑ Who looks like that? ❑ Health in all shapes and sizes ❑ Tricks of the trade

Notes

Lesson 31 Active Lifestyle: Endurance

There are three main elements to fitness: endurance (or cardio), strength (weight-bearing exercises), and flexibility (stretching). In the next few lessons, you'll find activities designed to help your child explore each of these aspects of physical fitness.

Kindergarten

Going farther than before

❑ **Counting hops**

Counting is a good way to encourage children to push themselves to build up endurance and cardiovascular health. If we stopped exercising every time we started to tire, our bodies would not maintain a high level of wellness. By making a game of counting while exercising, it's easier to keep going longer than we thought possible. Ask your child to choose an activity that can be done over and over, such as hopping, taking giant steps, doing frog leaps, etc. First, count how many hops (or steps or leaps) can be done in a certain amount of time, say 15 seconds. Next, have your child do that many hops, keeping track by counting. Choose another activity and do the same number, or add on. The goal here is to introduce the idea of keeping track of exercise by counting. The hidden benefit is a more sustained cardio workout resulting from having a target goal.

❑ **Family hike**

Take a family hike with the goal of going a little farther or a little longer than your child has done before. Another way to challenge your child's endurance is to find a hiking route that is steeper than usual or has more uneven footing. Explain beforehand that the hike will be more challenging to help everyone develop their hearts and lungs and that by developing endurance—the ability to keep going even after you might feel like stopping—we help our bodies grow stronger.

❑ **Red light, green light**

You are probably familiar with the game of Red Light, Green Light. One person (the caller) stands a distance away from the starting line where the players are lined up. The caller turns away from the players and calls out, "Green light!" This is the signal for the players to race towards the caller, trying to be the first one to touch him or her. The caller suddenly yells, "Red light!" and turns around. All players must stop and freeze in place at the command of "Red light." If the caller sees anyone still moving, that player gets sent back to the starting line. The caller turns around again and calls, "Green light!" and the game continues. This game is a fun way to build endurance because the game is so entertaining that players don't even notice how hard they are running.

Grade 1
Healthy heart and lungs

❑ **Measuring heart rate**

Help your child make a simple two-column chart. Write "Activity" at the top of the first column, and draw a heart at the top of the second column. Find a stop watch or clock with a second hand that you can use to record your child's heart rate after a series of activities. Begin by measuring the resting heart rate. Help your child find a good place to feel his or her pulse. Just under the jaw (the carotid artery) is a good place. If you have a stethoscope, you can use that. Count the number of beats in ten seconds, and then multiply it by six to find the heart-beats per minute (you might have to help with the math). Write down "at rest" in the first column, and record the heart rate in the second column. Next, have your child walk or march in place for 30 seconds and then measure the heart rate again (write "marching" on the chart and record the number of beats per minute). Then have your child do several more things (skipping, hopping, running, etc.) for 30 seconds each and record the heart rate. Alternate slower activities (such as stretching, taking baby steps, crawling on hands and knees, etc.) with faster ones and see how the heart rate changes. You might also do the exercises yourself and let your child measure and record your heart rate, listening at your chest if it's too difficult to detect the pulse at the neck or wrist.

- ❑ **Strong heart**

It's easy to forget that the heart is a muscle, but it is. That means it needs to be exercised to stay strong, just like any other muscle. Brainstorm with your child to create a fifteen- to thirty-minute cardio workout. Any activity that raises your heart rate is good. Let your child plan the workout and then the two of you do it together.

- ❑ **Belly breaths**

Just as the heart needs exercise, the lungs also benefit from breathing hard or with deep breaths. Belly breathing is a great way to bring your child's awareness to deep breathing. This can be done sitting, standing, or lying down. Take a deep breath—do this with your child as you give the instructions—and feel your lungs and ribcage expanding. Put your hands on your chest or ribs to feel it. As you keep breathing, imagine sending the breath down deeper into your body with each inhale. Breathe into your belly, putting your hands on it to feel it moving in and out. (Of course air isn't really going into the stomach, but the image of "breathing into the belly" helps the child engage the abdominals in moving air in and out of the lungs more actively.) You might even say, "Breathe all the way down into your legs. Let the breath go into your feet." End the exercise by instructing your child to just breathe normally. Discuss how deep breathing is very relaxing to the body, and it naturally occurs during exercise as the lungs expand to get more oxygen to the muscles.

Grade 2
Building stamina

- ❑ **Beat the clock**

The goal with this activity is to have your child try to improve his or her time in a physical challenge. You and your child can pick two or three activities, either from the list below or of your own choosing. Time the child with a stop watch or a clock with a second hand, and then have your child do several more trials, trying to improve his or her fastest time. Switch places and have your child time you and see if you can improve your time.

- do an obstacle course
- run a lap around the yard
- do speed walking
- run to point A, pick up an object, then run to point B, and put it down

❑ **Plus one**

Building stamina comes from pushing yourself to do a little more than you did the last time. Have your child choose a favorite activity and do it until tired (time it). The next day, repeat the activity and add one to it (one more minute, one more lap, one more block, etc.). Do the same thing the following day: add one more to the second day's total. Talk about how our amazing bodies can develop and improve, and how we can often do more than we think we can.

❑ **Last year/this year/next year**

Choose an activity your child enjoys doing, and have your child write down the skills that he or she could do last year. You might have to help with thinking back a whole year. Perhaps last year your child could ski the bunny slope, swim one pool length, or skateboard one block. Next, have your child write down where this ability or skill level stands today: skiing the green slopes, swimming two laps, or skating to the park. Finally, have your child write and/or draw what he or she hopes to be able to do one year from now. Encourage realistic expectations. You might like to join your child in this last year/this year/next year activity with goals of your own.

Grade 3

Aerobic and anaerobic exercise

❑ **Which is which?**

Explain the difference between aerobic and anaerobic activity by saying that an aerobic activity is one that makes your heart and lungs work hard but you can keep doing it for a long time. Anaerobic activity is something that works your heart and lungs as hard as they can, until you are gasping for breath, and you can only keep it up for a short time. Jogging is aerobic and sprinting is anaerobic. List as many different activities you can think of and ask your child to guess whether each is aerobic or anaerobic. Feel free to be a little silly with this. Here is a list to give you the idea:

aerobic: swimming with a friend

anaerobic: swimming away from a hungry shark

aerobic: doing high knee marching

anaerobic: doing jump knee tucks (jumping as high as you can while bringing your knees up to your chest—feel free to demonstrate)

aerobic: jumping rope with two hops per rotation

anaerobic: jumping rope "hot pepper" (one jump per rotation)

❑ **Sprinting heart rate**

Record your child's heart rate after walking a short distance (measure how many beats in ten seconds and then multiply that by six to get the beats per minute). Next, have your child go the same distance in a slow jog. Record the heart rate. Then have your child do it at a normal run, and record the heart rate. Finally have your child go the distance sprinting at a flat out run, as fast as possible. Record the heart rate and while your child walks to bring the heart rate and breathing back to normal, talk about the difference between aerobic and anaerobic exercises.

❑ **Dance party**

It's easy to work up a sweat (and heightened heart rate and breathing) while dancing. It'll help if you join your child in this fun activity. Begin by dancing at a moderate speed for about a minute (for example, one step per beat), and then suddenly speed up, dancing double time (two steps for each beat). After 30 seconds or so, slow down to regular speed, but keep moving. Then suddenly shift into slow motion (one step for every two beats). After 30 seconds or so, speed back up to the normal rhythm. Continue to move from fast forward to slo-mo a few more times. This can just be done for fun (your child will feel the difference internally even if you don't discuss it) or you can talk afterwards about how your hearts and lungs reacted to dancing at different speeds.

Lesson 32 Active Lifestyle: Strength

The second element of physical fitness is strength training or weight-bearing exercises. This includes any exercise that involves pushing, pulling, or holding up your own body weight. Push-ups, pull-ups (chin-ups) and sit-ups are good examples. This lesson presents a variety of ways to incorporate strength training into your child's daily activities.

Kindergarten
Show your muscles

❑ **Relative strength**

Our bodies have muscles of all shapes and sizes. This activity is a playful exploration of relative muscle strength. Begin by searching for objects in the house that can be moved with one finger. Can your child move a can of soup with one finger? Can one finger move a potted plant? Is the pinky finger as strong as the thumb? Keep experimenting until you find something too heavy to move with a finger, and then get both hands involved (which will include the arms and shoulders). Can your child push a chair with two hands? Can two hands push the couch? Keep a close eye on your child to make sure he or she isn't going to strain muscles or push something that can fall over. When you find something too heavy to push with two hands, see if using two legs will move the object—sit on the floor with hands braced behind you, put your feet on the object and use your leg muscles to push. You and your child can do this together to ensure that your child isn't going to overdo it and get hurt. Your child will probably discover that leg muscles are stronger than arm muscles (you might point out that leg muscles are also bigger than arm muscles) and that arm muscles are stronger than finger muscles.

❑ Arm wrestle

Arm wrestling is a fun game even if you are wrestling against someone stronger than you. It is a great strength training exercise. Teach your child the basics:

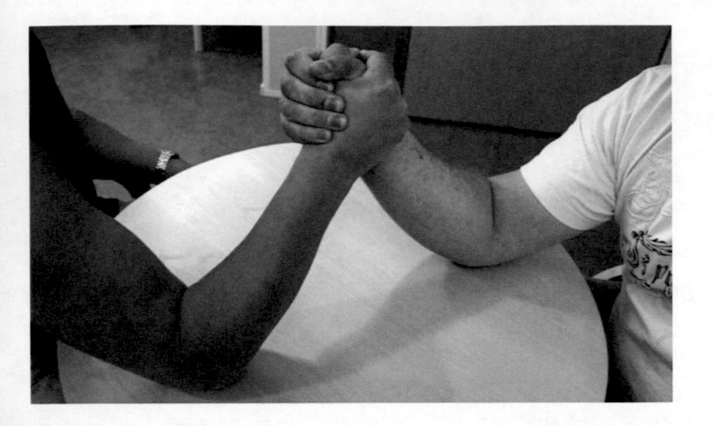

1. Face each other seated across a table, with right elbows on the table.
2. Grasp right hands together, and hold your left hands together between your elbows, left forearms flat on the table.
3. Count to three and then try to push your partner's arm down to touch the table.

Once your child gets the hang of arm wrestling with you, have him or her challenge friends and family. Remember to switch hands and wrestle with your left hand as well. Your child might be surprised to find out one arm is much stronger than the other. (If you know how to thumb wrestle, that's fun to do, too.)

❑ Together we stand

This exercise works best with two people who are close in size, but you and your child can try it as well. Sit on the floor, back to back, with your legs out in front of you, knees bent. Link arms on both sides. Pushing against one another's back, slowly try to stand without letting go of your arms. This takes a surprising amount of leg strength. The harder you push against one another, the easier it will be to stand.

Grade 1
How to grow stronger

❑ Push yourself

If you have a rolling chair, skateboard, piano dolly, or other flat rolling cart, here's a great way to exercise using wheels.

- Rolling chair: Have your child sit in the rolling chair and move around the room using only leg strength. Afterwards, you can sit in the chair and have your child push you around (you might have to reciprocate!).
- Skateboard or flat cart: Have your child sit on the dolly and

use leg muscles to push and maneuver around. If it is safe, your child can also lie down with his or her stomach on the dolly and use arms to maneuver around.

For an added challenge, create a simple obstacle course to wheel around.

❑ **Crabs and frogs**

Imitating animals is fun, funny, and great exercise.

- Crab walk: Teach your child how to crab walk (sit on the ground and use hands and feet to raise buttocks off the ground, then crawl forward, backward, or sideways). Have crab walk races, or do crab walk obstacle courses that require moving in multiple directions.

- Frog jumps: Leap like a frog (starting and ending in a low squat with hands on the ground and knees out to the side). See how high you can leap and how far you can go in one leap. Pick a destination and race one another there using frog jumps.

❑ **Be your own cheerleader**

Everyone needs a little encouragement at some point, and learning how to give yourself a pep talk or be your own cheerleader can help you keep going when you feel like giving up. Take turns with your child, coming up with catchy, encouraging phrases, like, "I can do it! I can do it!" or "I'm climbing to the top, and I'm never going to stop!" or simply chant your name with the word *go*: "Go, Jordan! Go, Jordan!" Chant each phrase in rhythm while exercising. The next time one of you needs a little encouragement, be your own cheerleader.

Grade 2

Muscle groups

❑ **Push me-pull you pairs**

Just like the silly imaginary creature in Hugh Lofting's *Doctor Doolittle* books (a deer-like animal with two heads and a joined body, each half always going in the opposite direction), our bodies have muscle pairs that can work together or against one another. Here are two exercises that highlight these opposing muscle groups.

- Biceps/triceps: The main muscles on the upper arm (the biceps on the front of the arm and the triceps on the back of the arm) are primarily responsible for bending and straightening the elbow. Have your child try to feel these muscles working by placing one hand on the muscle of the other arm while bending and straightening the arm. Once he or she can feel the biceps and triceps, try this exercise. Have your child bend the elbow and make a fist, and you hold the fist in your hand. Now have your child alternately bend (flexing the bicep) and straighten the arm (flexing the triceps) while you provide resistance by making it hard for the arm to move. Do this a few times, making your child work hard enough to feel these two muscles. Switch places and have your child try to hold your fist still while you alternately flex biceps and triceps.
- Quadriceps/hamstrings: These two large muscles of the thigh (quads on the front and hamstrings on the back) are active in lifting, bending, and straightening the leg. Have your child try to feel these muscles working in the leg by touching them while lifting the knee (activating the quad) and lifting the heel to the buttocks (activating the hamstring). Provide some resistance by pushing down on the thigh while your child tries to raise the knee, or by pushing down on the heel while your child tries to raise it.

❑ **Follow the leader**

Play a game of Follow the Leader with each of you taking turns leading different exercises that test and develop your strength, such as push-ups against a wall, leg lifts, or sit-ups. Try to include exercises for all parts of the body.

❑ **The main muscle groups**

This activity encourages your child to experiment with making up exercises that will use each of the three main muscle groups: legs, arms/shoulders/chest, and core (abs and back). Talk about the muscles involved and what they do, and then see how many exercises you and your child can come up with to work these different muscles groups. If you get stumped, you can search for ideas in exercise books or online.

Grade 3

Care of muscle bruises, strains, and sprains

❑ **Body check**

Paying attention to the body helps us detect when something is not quite right. In the course of daily living or during exercise, it's easy to become injured with a twisted ankle, a fall, or a bump. Teach your child to do a body check by naming body parts from head to toe and taking a few moments to focus on that part (either mentally or by physically touching it). Tell your child to be on the lookout for anything that hurts or feels different (limited range of motion, for example). If something hurts, try to figure out why. Ask, "Can you remember what happened?" or "Did you trip and fall?" The goal of this activity is not to diagnose or treat injuries, but to emphasize the importance of being aware of the body and to pay attention to injuries (rather than ignoring them) and seek treatment when necessary.

❑ **R.I.C.E.**

This activity introduces your child to the basic care of minor injuries to muscles and joints. You might have learned that R.I.C.E. stands for Rest, Ice, Compression, and Elevation. The Red Cross has recently revised their practices, and now are teaching Rest, Immobilize, Cold, and Elevate. Have your child practice self-care by pretending he or she has twisted an ankle and it is now swollen and hurting

Rest: Stop using the ankle. Your child might limp or hop around.

Immobilize: Stabilize the injured area so it doesn't move around.

Cold: Apply ice for a few minutes by putting an ice pack (or ice cubes in a plastic bag) in a towel and putting it on the ankle to reduce the swelling and pain.

Elevation: Elevate the ankle above the heart (if possible) by putting it up on a chair or lying on the couch and propping it up with pillows (only do this if it does not cause more pain).

R.I.C.E. can also be applied to an imaginary injured elbow, wrist, knee, or any body part that can be rested, immobilized, iced, and elevated. Your child might also like to practice R.I.C.E. by treating an "injured" stuffed animal.

❑ **Wrap it up (mummy me)**

Practicing a bandage wrap is as practical as it is fun. If possible, use a real elastic Ace bandage. If you don't have one, any long strip of stretchy cloth will do. (You can cut an old tee-shirt into one long strip by doing one long spiral cut, starting at the hem and going round and round.) Supervise this activity to encourage safety, checking to make sure bandages are not wrapped tight enough to inhibit blood flow. If extremities are turning red or purple, circulation is being cut off and bandages should be loosened immediately. If you know how to wrap a bandage correctly (as taught in most first aid courses), you can teach the proper technique. If not, don't worry—this activity can still be enjoyable and useful. Take turns having fake injuries and applying a bandage wrap. It's a good idea for your child to experience what a wrap feels like, and to practice the skill of wrapping.

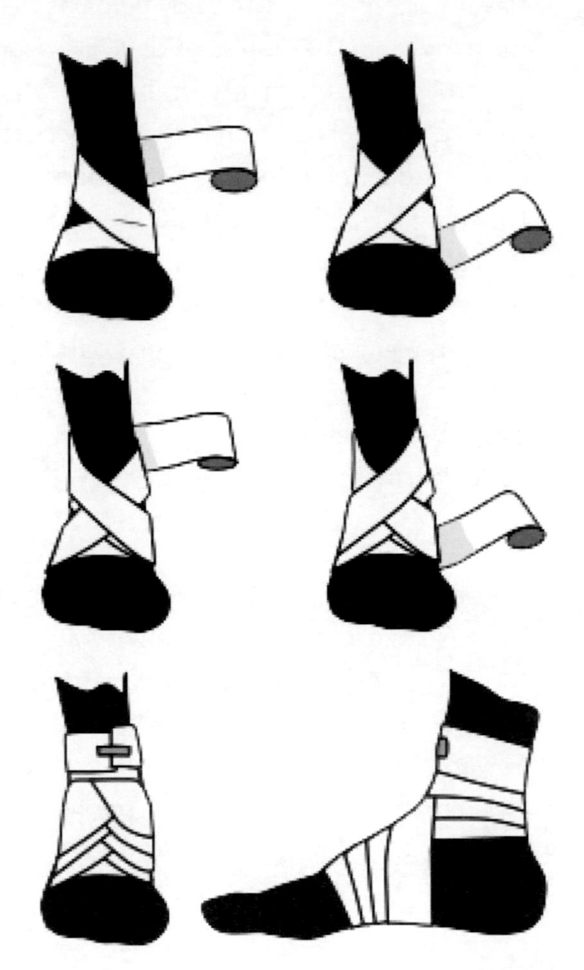

Lesson 33 Active Lifestyle: Flexibility

Keeping muscles and joints supple and flexible may seem unnecessary for children, who normally are very flexible. However, stretching exercises are just as beneficial to young bodies as to older ones. Besides, stretching feels wonderful and is a great way to start the day, or to unwind and relax.

Kindergarten

Stretch and bend

❑ **Twisting and turning**

This is free-form activity that focuses on loosening up joints through range-of-motion movements. Start with circling your wrists several times in each direction, and then do arm circles in each direction. Swing the arms forward and back, clapping hands in front and behind. Keep moving through different body parts, gently twisting and turning the spine, hips, knees, ankles, and neck. Model gentle loose movements—this should feel easy and smooth, not hard and abrupt.

❑ **Trees in the wind**

Stand facing one another with arms held out or above your head. Pretend you are trees in the wind. You can make whooshing noises to help make it easier to pretend. Begin with a gentle breeze, swaying side to side, moving your "branches" (arms) slowly. Increase the wind speed so that the top of your trunk (ribs, arms, and shoulders) is moving further from side to side, bending and twisting with a larger range of motion. Finally, have the wind turn into a storm, moving your whole tree trunk in all directions. Keep the feet ("roots") in place, but let the knees, hips, and spine get involved. After a minute of bending and twisting in the wild wind, have the wind slowly die down, until eventually your tree is standing still and calm.

❑ **How tall? How far?**

Ask your child a series of questions that he or she can answer without words, stretching the body to demonstrate the answer with movements. Here are a few questions to start you off—think of as many as you can.

- How high can you reach?
- How far can your arms reach from side to side?
- How wide is your hand?
- How big of a step can you take?
- With your hands at your sides, how far down your leg can you reach if you bend sideways?
- Can you touch your fingers or palms to the floor while keeping your legs straight?

Grade 1
What are you stretching and why?

❑ **Muscle changes**

As you stretch, your muscles become more elastic. This amazing ability can be measured with this simple activity. Have your child sit on the ground in a straddle position (legs in a V shape). Place a small item, like a small stone or a block, directly in front of your child and say, "Bend forward with a straight back and straight legs and push the stone as far away from you as your fingers will reach. Don't push past the point where your leg muscles hurt." Once this is done, mark the spot on the ground where the stone is (use chalk, a piece of tape, or another stone marker). Have your child spend the next few minutes gently stretching the leg muscles. The buttocks need to stay in the same spot, but the legs can bend and open and close. Demonstrate stretches such as touching the toes, doing a seated side stretch, and pulling in one foot and stretching one leg at a time. After a few minutes of stretching, have your child resume a straddle position (with the buttocks in the original spot) and push the stone as far as possible. Did it go farther this time? Talk about why.

❑ **Flex and Snap**

Muscles have the ability to expand and contract a great deal without harm. However, muscles can sometimes tear when overused or when used without adequate warm up. To demonstrate this, find several sticks, some dry and some fresh (green). Talk about how muscles can be very flexible, and bend and flex the green sticks and see how far they can bend without breaking. Then explain that when muscles are cold or haven't been used in a while, they can be stiff and prone to injury. Break a few dry sticks to demonstrate (of course, muscles don't actually break in the same way sticks do, but the implication is that they will be seriously injured). Experiment with a few warm-up exercises (such as marching in place while swinging the arms) while you discuss ways to protect muscles from injury.

❑ **Before and after**

This activity focuses on how the range of motion is affected by exercise. Have your child stand on one leg and grasp the other knee, pulling it as high as possible. Measure the distance between the knee and the chest. Next, do a few minutes of leg swings and leg circles (draw a circle on the floor with your toe, making it bigger and bigger with each rotation). Change the direction of the circles, and keep loosening up the hip joint. After a few minutes, bring the knee to the chest again. Did it come closer this time? As an adult, your results from this exercise will probably be even more dramatic than your child's since children have a great deal of natural flexibility. Have your child try to guess why this change occurred, and discuss how the body's abilities change as flexibility improves. As you do a warm-up (light exercise done in preparation for more strenuous activity), the blood flow to your muscles increases along with their temperature, and muscles become more elastic, which in turn allows them to contract and expand more smoothly and move joints more efficiently.

Grade 2

Yoga

❑ **Animal poses**

Yoga poses can increase circulation, improve flexibility, and bring a calm sense of focus and well-being. Try these yoga poses with your child. Move slowly into and out of the poses, and hold each pose for a few breaths.

- Cobra: lie on the floor face down with hands under your shoulders. Push your upper body away from the floor until you are looking up toward the sky. Keep the belly button, hips, and legs on the floor.
- Cat and cow: Start on your hands and knees with your head looking at the floor (so your spine is straight). Pull the belly button toward the spine until your back curves like a cat arching. and your chin tucks under. Slowly release, and then bend the spine in the opposite direction until your chin tilts upward, like a sway-backed cow with its belly hanging down. Slowly release.
- Eagle: Begin in a standing position. Wrap your right leg around your left, letting your left knee bend slightly, while wrapping your arms around each other until the palms are touching. Try to keep your balance while you hold the position and then slowly unwind. Repeat on the other side.

❑ **Sun salute**

Here is a simple adaptation of the traditional Sun Salutation. Move slowly through the poses, taking time for two to five breaths in each position.

1. Stand straight with palms together in front of the chest (prayer position).
2. Raise the hands above the head.
3. Bend at the waist until hands are touching the toes.
4. Lift the upper body halfway to standing until you have a flat back, with hands on knees (table-top position or upside down L).
5. Bend down to touch the toes again, and place hands on the

floor.

6. Step back into plank position (like you are going to do a push-up).
7. Bend arms and slowly lower the stomach to the floor.
8. Push the arms straight, raising the upper body and tilting the face up toward the sky (hips and legs stay relaxed on the ground).
9. Return to plank position.
10. Step feet to hands and return to standing.

❑ **Balance poses**

Yoga balance poses provide an excellent challenge that requires core strength and focus. Try these in a place where there is plenty of room and a soft surface (rug or grass) in case your child topples (or you do!). Balance poses should be done very slowly. Focus your eyes on a fixed point in front of you to help maintain your concentration and balance. If your child enjoys these yoga positions, explore more by taking a class or checking out a book or video.

- Tree pose: Begin standing straight with palms together in front of the chest. Stand on your right foot and bring your left foot to rest on the inside of your right knee. Your left knee will point out to the side. Slowly raise your hands, with palms touching, until they are reaching straight above your head. If your balance is stable, slowly open your arms wide until they are pointing up in a wide V (like branches of a tree). Reverse the movements to come out of the pose and back to standing. Repeat on the other foot.
- King Dancer pose: Stand on your right leg, and bend your left knee to raise your heel toward your buttocks. Grasp your left ankle with your left hand and raise your right hand straight above your head. Stand as tall and straight as you can. If your balance is stable, lean forward slowly while reaching forward

with your right hand and pulling your left leg up behind you. You will be making a T shape with your body. Slowly reverse the motions to come back to standing, and then repeat on the other side.

Grade 3

Warm up and cool down

❑ **Wiggle and flex**

It's a good idea to get in the habit of warming up before exercise. Here is a head-to-toe warm-up that loosens and flexes each joint and muscle group. Do each exercise several times—don't rush it. This can be done in about three to five minutes.

Head/neck:

- look right and left
- tilt ear to shoulder
- look up and down

Shoulders:

- arm circles forward and backwards
- hug yourself and then open arms wide
- lift shoulders and drop them

Arms/wrists:

- wrist circles
- press palms together
- shake arms and swing them back and forth

Spine:

- swing arms left to wrap around the body and look over the left shoulder (repeat on right)
- with hands on thighs, round the back and then release
- bend sideways with one hand reaching down and one hand reaching overhead

Hips/knees:

- put hands on hips and circle hips in both directions

- put hands on knees and circle knees in both directions
- lift knee and clasp it to the chest

Ankles/feet:

- circle ankles in both directions
- flex and point the toes
- raise up on tip toe

❑ **Sweat spots**

Sweat is an important sign. It shows that you have worked your body hard enough to heat up (sweat is the body's way of cooling off) and that you are not dehydrated. Different people sweat at different rates, even if they are exercising at the same intensity, and some children do not sweat very much until they reach puberty. Have your child do this test to see how much sweat is being produced. After vigorous exercise, cut a paper napkin into four squares (or use a thin cloth). Press a square onto the skin at each of the following places on the body where sweat often accumulates and see if sweat leaves a wet spot.

- forehead
- back of the neck (under the hair)
- under the arm
- have your child find one other place (between the shoulder blades, small of the back, upper lip, feet, etc.)

You might want to talk about sweat being a natural process of the human body and that antiperspirants, which are designed to inhibit perspiring, go against the body's natural (and necessary) process. You can explain the difference between antiperspirants and deodorants (deodorants are designed to prevent or cover up underarm odor, but not to inhibit the sweating process). You might want to explain the importance of changing out of sweaty clothes to avoid skin irritation, or discuss the importance of showering to remove dried sweat and dirt after exercising.

❑ **After exercise**

After exercising long enough and hard enough to raise the heart rate and breathing, it's good to keep moving while the body cools down. Create a two- to three-minute cool-down routine with your child to help the body get back to normal. You can use this guideline or make up one of your own.

- Walk around until the heart rate and breathing normalize.
- Shake the arms and legs gently to help relax the muscles and release any tension.
- Stretch, bend, and twist, using each of the major muscle groups (legs, arms/shoulders/chest, and core/abs/back).
- Take a deep breath while stretching arms overhead. Repeat a few times.
- Drink a glass of water to rehydrate (replace fluids).

Lesson 34 Body, Mind, and Spirit

With high-level wellness, the body, mind, and spirit are brought into balance. The human body is enhanced by a healthy mind and spirit; the human mind is fueled by a vigorous body and spirit; and the human spirit is nurtured by a strong mind and body. Everything is connected. This lesson's activities help your child explore the connections between body, mind, and spirit.

Kindergarten

Kindness and affirmations

❑ **Kind thoughts, kind words**

Many adults have a plethora of negative thoughts running through their heads on a daily basis—"I'm not good enough; I can't do that; what a dumb thing I said or did"—so it's no surprise that children can easily fall into negative thought patterns, as well. If you notice your child using negative self-talk (speaking about him- or herself in a negative or self-defeating manner), you can offer options of alternative language: "I can't do that" can be changed to "That's challenging for me" or "I can try." Whether or not negative thought patterns are developing, learning to use affirmations effectively can change attitudes in a very positive way. With your child's help, come up with three positive statements that reflect abilities or attitudes your child wants to develop. Write these statements in the present tense, as though they are already true. Here are a few possibilities:

- I am a patient big sister.
- I am helpful around the house.
- I can learn to do anything.
- I can always come up with great ideas.

Write down three statements of your choice and have your child decorate them, and then display them where they can be seen often and spoken aloud to reinforce this positive outlook.

❑ **It's all about attitude**

Attitude plays a very important role in sickness, healing, and health. In this simple exercise, your child will have the opportunity to experience how easily our bodies can respond to the messages our brains convey. Have your child lie down on the floor, face up. Ask your child to raise one leg at a time and then put it down. Next, ask your child to imagine a huge weight pressing down on the legs, not painfully, but like a very heavy blanket so the legs feel like they weigh a ton. Take a minute to describe this while your child imagines it. Now have your child raise and lower one leg at a time. Was it harder to do? Finally, ask your child to imagine his or her legs feeling light as a feather, like they could just float on air. Spend a minute describing this feeling, and then ask your child to lift each leg once more. Was
it easier?

You might relate this to how having a positive or negative attitude can affect behavior and physical responses. For instance, if a child is convinced that a new food will taste terrible, the gag reflex can be triggered even before the food is smelled. Likewise, if a child believes that a new food will taste delicious, the food is more likely to be tried with an open mind.

❑ **Active relaxation**

Most people feel more inclined to a positive outlook when they have opportunities for relaxation in their lives. The body doesn't necessarily need to be physically resting in order for it to reap the benefits that come from relaxation. A deep sense of satisfaction and calm can come when the body is at rest and the mind is active (as in reading or doing a puzzle), or when the body is active and the mind is at rest (as in running or swimming). Active relaxation can also be found when both the mind and body are engaged, as when doing any craft, hobby, artistic activity, or other favorite pursuit: horseback riding, knitting, model construction, hiking, etc. Just about any activity that brings a feeling of well-being can fall into the category of active relaxation. See if your child can create a list of activities that are both relaxing and active, and then choose one to do each day.

Grade 1
Mind and health

❑ The energy of thought

Learning to send thought energy into an area of the body that needs help may sound like mumbo-jumbo to some, but this activity can be beneficial and enjoyable whether or not it is believed to be effective. The science behind the idea is that by engaging the brain with intention, physical changes in the body can occur. Follow the steps below, doing them with your child as you give the instructions.

1. Lie in a comfortable position with eyes closed.
2. Take a few deep breaths and bring your attention to your body. Feel if there are any places that feel tight or hurt.
3. Imagine your heart as a strong, warm, red heart shape in the center of your chest, or as a bright yellow sun. Imagine it sending healing warmth into your body with each breathe you take.
4. Feel this wonderful, relaxing warmth spread out into your body, filling your chest and stomach, spreading into your arms and legs, all the way down into your hands and feet like warm, smooth, slow-moving honey.
5. Let this warmth fill your body and melt away any areas of tension.
6. After a few minutes, slowly open your eyes.

Ask your child if he or she felt any changes, or felt differently afterward.

❑ Biofeedback

Biofeedback is a technique where you develop an awareness of bodily sensations (especially those related to stress or illness, such as an elevated heart rate or the onset of a tension headache) and you learn to counteract the symptoms by using the mind to help the body heal itself. This activity allows your child to explore how biofeedback works. First, record your child's heart rate (count the beats in ten seconds and multiply by six for the heart rate per minute). Use a stethoscope, if you have one, and let your child listen. Next, tell your child to try to slow the heart down by thinking of the heart beats calming down as they do when the body is asleep. Give your child a minute to imagine this. You can either continue guiding your child with gentle instructions or let your child do this silently. Check the heart rate again (and let your child listen) and report if there were any changes. Then tell your child to try to speed up the heart rate, just by thinking about doing something exciting or fast paced. Check the rate again after a minute, and report the results. Talk about ways biofeedback techniques might be useful.

❑ **Following your gut**

The expression "follow your gut" refers to intuition, but the digestive process can also give us helpful information about our health. If something worries us, we may feel an upset stomach or our appetite can be altered, making us feel more or less like eating. The "gut instinct" can help us make better decisions. The next time your child is faced with an ethical or moral decision, ask, "What does your heart say? What does your mind say? What does your gut say?" If there is conflict between mind and heart, or a sense of unfairness, or if the decision is somehow wrong, the gut will often respond with a feeling of tension, queasiness, or even pain. Learning to listen to this gut feeling, rather than ignore it, will serve your child well.

Grade 2
Body and spirit

❑ **Spiritual beliefs**

Many people feel very strongly that human beings have an essence that transcends the physical body. This spiritual presence can be nurtured in many different ways, through religious traditions, meditation or prayer, or communing with nature, to name a few. A healthy spiritual life lends vitality and strength to our overall well-being. Take this opportunity to share with your child the spiritual beliefs of your family, if you have any, and talk about the ways in which your family nurtures a healthy spiritual connection.

❑ **Intuition and following your path**

Animals in the wild have a strong intuitive sense that keeps them safe and guides them through life. In this activity, your child will choose one or more animals to study and learn about their instinctive behavior. For instance, migrating birds and fish will follow an unseen path to a faraway nesting or spawning site. Mammals will instinctively nurse without being taught, and turtle hatchlings navigate through the sand to the water and begin swimming and feeding without any instruction.

Talk about the difference between instinct and intuition. Humans have very few instincts, but our intuition can be a very powerful tool that guides our steps throughout life.

- ❑ **Daily reminders**

Many people enjoy a daily spiritual reminder that provides a word or phrase to focus on throughout the day. Perhaps this might be a religious verse or an "angel card" (a set of cards naming life-affirming attributes). Another lovely way to use spiritual reminders is to create a set of spirit stones. These are simple polished rocks that have a single word painted on each, words such as hope, faith, peace, courage, love, believe, purpose, possibility, abundance, wisdom, balance, strength, trust, compassion, and gratitude. Help your child create a set of spirit stones for your home. Keep them in a bowl or basket and choose one each day. Talk about ways in which this spiritual attribute might be expressed in daily life.

Grade 3
Healing touch

- ❑ **Foot reflexology**

Reflexology is an ancient art that uses touch to stimulate reflex points on the body (usually in the feet and hands) in order to promote health and healing of the body organs, structures, and systems. While the field of reflexology is vast and complex, it's easy to learn and practice a few simple techniques. Demonstrate these on your child, and then your child can practice on you—a win-win situation! It's best to relax while receiving reflexology (or any healing touch) rather than to do simultaneous foot massages with your child. Here are a few basic strokes:

Applying firm pressure in a single spot using thumb, finger, or knuckle

Kneading using a circular motion

Tapping with fingers, fists, or cupped palms

Brushing using fingertips in a sweeping motion

Jiggling with a finger or hand on a contact point (do not rub)

Inching along by rolling from the ball of the thumb to the tip

To begin, have your child lie down in a comfortable position, and then position yourself so you can easily work on the feet. You can use lotion or massage oil if you'd like, but it isn't necessary. Take your time with each stroke, repeating it as many times as you'd like. Make sure to treat each foot to the same tender loving care.

1. Rub your hands briskly to warm them up and then gently touch the feet. Rest your hands on the feet without moving for a few breaths to help you and your child relax into the sensation.

2. Mold your hands to the contours of the foot. You can work on one foot at a time or on both feet together, whichever you prefer. Begin rubbing your hands gently over the entire foot, top and bottom, for a minute or so. Breathe slowly and deeply and move your hands in tune with your breathing. Let your hands feel where to go by following the shape of the foot.

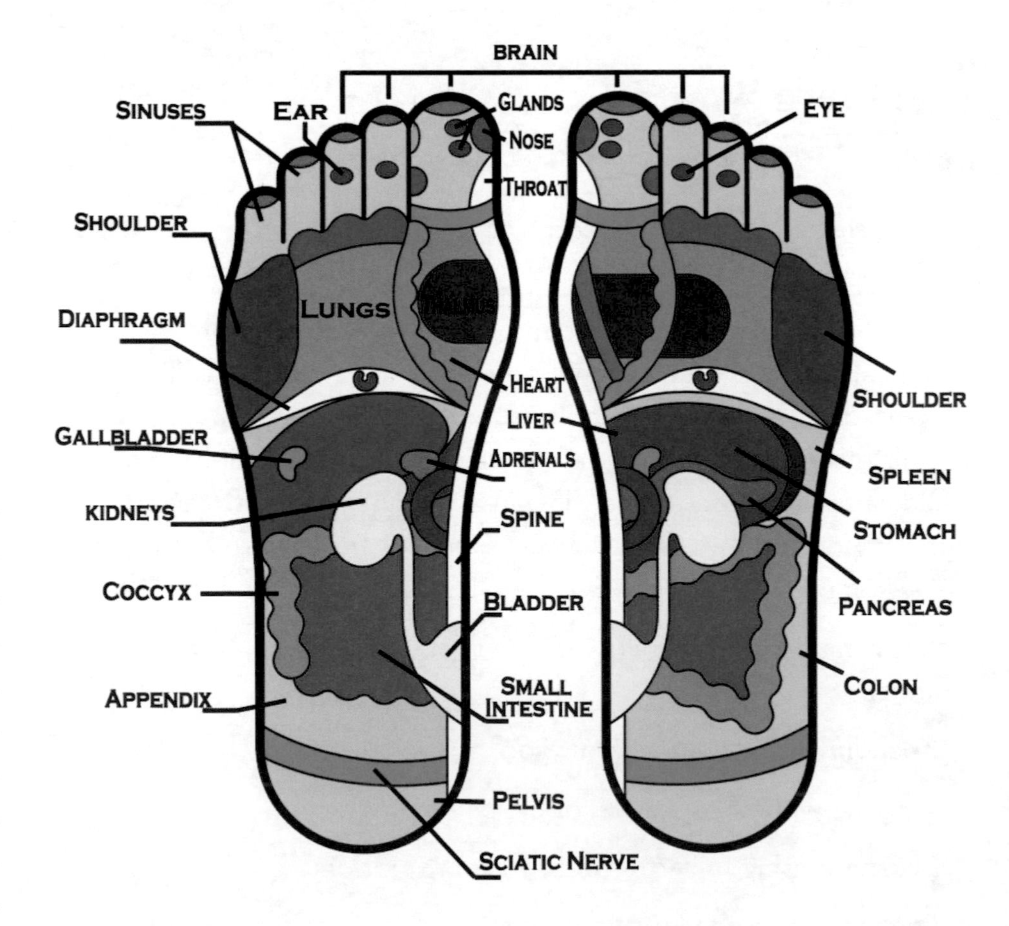

3. Using two hands on one foot, wring the foot gently as though you are wringing out a sponge. Rotate your hands back and forth, wringing the whole foot, moving from the heel up to the toes.
4. Use your fingers to "walk" along the outer edge of the foot from heel to little toe.
5. Squeeze the pad of each toe. Gently rotate each toe.
6. Experiment with other touches, pressure points, and strokes, according to what feels needed and what feels good to your child.
7. Complete the reflexology session by tapping or brushing your fingers over the whole surface of the foot (top and bottom) and then give one final firm stroke along the length of the foot from heel to toe. Shake your hands to release any residual tension or energy.

If your child is interested in learning more about reflexology, you can get a book from the library or find information online. Have your child draw a foot map, labeling each part of the foot with its corresponding body part.

❑ **Massage**

Massage, like reflexology, is an ancient, complex, and highly-effective form of healing touch. Explore the art of massage with your child by following the instructions for reflexology above, but focusing on larger body areas (such as shoulder and neck, back, legs, or arms and hands) or on the entire body. You can adapt the six basic strokes listed above to any area of the body, and follow the reflexology techniques in steps one to four for a general body massage. Experiment with what feels needed and what feels good. Feel free to find a book on massage to explore this healing art more fully.

- ❑ **Animals and touch**

Many pets enjoy massage as much as humans do. Stroking a pet often produces a sense of tranquility in human beings. If you have a willing pet, have your child experiment with animal massage. Remind your child to stroke the pet very gently at first, and to repeat strokes a few times, always moving slowly and in the direction of the fur. Watch your pet for signs of relaxation or discomfort, and help your child learn to "read" the animal's behavioral signs. Remind your child to breathe slowly and let the hands feel the shapes of bones, muscles, and joints under the skin. Allow these shapes to guide the direction of the strokes.

Lesson 35 Mindfulness and Well-Being

In modern times, stress can come into our lives in many forms. Developing mindfulness techniques that enhance personal harmony and inner balance will serve your child well for the rest of his or her life. Mindfulness refers to the ability to be fully present in the moment, without worrying about the past or planning for the future. Learning how to simply be present in a quiet, focused way can have wide ranging benefits for the body, mind, and spirit.

Kindergarten
Balance and stillness

❑ **Balancing act**

Balance can be found on many levels: physical, mental, and emotional, as well as balance in outward and inward activities, rest and action, talking and listening, work and play. This exercise uses physical balance to help your child tune into the inner sensations of the body, focusing the mind in order to feel what's going on inside. Use a seesaw, balance board, or improvised plank on a log, and ask your child to straddle the center and find the balance point. You may need to hold your child's hand to guard against a loss of balance. If possible, have your child find the balance point on more than one type of structure. If this is too easy, have your child try to stay in balance while doing a squat or lifting up his or her arms. This activity of tuning into the sense of inner (physical) balance can open up pathways toward inner mental and

emotional balance that are the goal of more advanced mindfulness techniques.

❑ **Stillness**

Stillness is often not part of an active child's day—sometimes it seems like children never stop moving until they are asleep! This activity uses sitting still to introduce the concept of a still mind. Have your child find a comfortable sitting position on the floor across from you (you'll do this activity together). Place a bell or chime on the ground before you, if you have one, or some other instrument that makes a music tone (you can use a timer if you don't have anything else). Explain that when you ring the bell, you will both close your eyes and sit as still as possible until the bell rings again. You will just sit quietly and breathe deeply. Notice the way the air feels moving through the nostrils, cool air coming in and warm air going out. Notice the belly rising and falling. Instruct your child to try to focus on breathing in and out, that's all. If any other thoughts come into mind, just keep going back to paying attention to the breathing. Ring the bell after only about 30 seconds of quiet sitting—you want the first session to be successful.

If your child was fidgety during the 30 seconds, afterward you might say something like, "I almost moved when my nose itched but then I remembered I was trying to sit as still as a rock. Were you able to sit still the whole time?" or "My mind kept racing about what I'm going to do later today, but I kept trying to just go back to thinking about breathing in and breathing out. Did that happen to you?" Try the exercise again and try to increase the time of stillness, if your child seems ready for it. Repeat this activity once or twice each day for a week and see if your child's ability to achieve a state of stillness improves.

❑ **Gratitude game**

This is a wonderful activity to incorporate into your daily bedtime routine. It is a simple exercise where you and your child take turns speaking aloud the things you are grateful for in your lives. You can frame this in any way you like. Here are a few possibilities:

"I love..."

"Name three good things that happened today."

"I'm thankful for..."

"Name three things you are grateful for."

"I appreciate..."

Ask your child to notice where in the body he or she feels gratitude. This helps your child realize that gratitude is more than just words; it is a feeling in the body as well as a particular frame of mind.

Grade 1

Inner awareness

❑ **At the sound of the bell**

In this activity, you will use a bell to signal a moment of silent contemplation. Find a bell or singing bowl with a nice, rich tone. Explain to your child that whenever someone rings the bell or strikes the bowl, you'll use that as a signal to stop what you are doing and focus on a moment of stillness. Close your eyes and take a deep breath as you just focus on the sound of the bell until it fades away completely. You may want to get into the habit of ringing the bell at each meal, after everyone is seated at the table but before eating begins. After practicing a moment of stillness, you might want to suggest adding a phrase that can be repeated silently while the bell sound is echoing. Phrases such as, "I am grateful for all that I have" or "Love is all around me" can bring an overall sense of tranquility and well-being.

❑ **One word**

It can be beneficial to focus on one word while doing a breathing or stillness exercise. You and your child can experiment with how it feels to repeat one word or phrase silently in your mind while taking five deep breaths, or while doing a simple yoga stretch or pose, or while sitting quietly before bedtime. Depending on the situation, you might use one of the following words: peaceful, relax, happiness, love. Guide your child in this technique by reminding him or her to repeat the word and focus all thoughts on the word: how it sounds, what it means, how it feels, what it represents. It can be helpful to repeat the word in rhythm with the breathing. For instance, two-syllable words can be expanded to take one whole breath (inhale while thinking the first syllable and exhale on the second syllable). Instruct your child to let the word breathe in and out of his or her mind slowly. This can be done with eyes closed or while focusing on a candle flame or a beautiful or meaningful object that brings the word to mind.

❏ **Make your own**

Many people who use meditation and mindfulness techniques develop their own personal routines and patterns of thought that work for them. In this activity, you will offer your child a range of choices and let him or her figure out what works best. You and your child might try different combinations of activities, such as two or more of the following: ringing a bell, deep breathing, repeating a word, watching a candle (supervised, of course), humming while breathing out, visualization, etc. You might want to create a simple mindfulness routine that can be used at regular times (such as before meals or before bed) or whenever your child needs to focus inwardly to find a renewed sense of balance.

Grade 2
Deepening the connection

❏ **Inside, outside, and upside down**

Sometimes it is helpful to change our physical position or surroundings in order to achieve a clearer sense of being present in the moment. Begin this activity by sitting down in a comfortable position. Ask your child to listen to what's going on around him or her, the normal daily sounds of life. (It might be easier to focus on sounds with eyes closed.) Your child doesn't have to say anything, just listen. After a minute or so, ask your child to focus on what's going on inside of him or her. Just listen to the inner thoughts and any bodily noises, such as the breath or the sound of swallowing. Again, nothing needs to be said. Just listen. After a few minutes, move to a new location or a new position. You might move outside, or go sit beside a stream, or lie down, or hang upside down off the side of the couch. See how this new position or location changes things. Listen to what is going on outside the body and then to what is going on inside the body. The goal is simply to focus on quieting the mind and body and bringing awareness to the moment.

❏ **Breathing and visualization**

This activity introduces breathing and visualization techniques that can help bring focus and a sense of presence and tranquility to the moment. There are many ways to use breathing, meditation, and visualization to relax, and many excellent books on the topic. You may have a favorite technique—by all means, use it—or you may want to try one of these:

- Sit or lie down comfortably (both you and your child). Quietly talk your child through a few minutes of deep breathing. Breathe in for the count of three, hold one second, and then breathe out for the count of five. If this seems too forced or unnatural, just say, "Take a deep breath and count to yourself as you let it out all the way." You might feel like doing a full body stretch, too.
- Sit or lie down comfortably, and tell your child that you'll do a simple meditation for a few minutes. Talk your child through the following activity. Take a deep breath so that it feels like there's a big balloon inside you filling you up and making you feel light inside. As you let out your breath, make a sound like a hum or like a whooshing wind. Continue to breathe in like a balloon and out with a hum or a whoosh. Do this for a few breaths and then just lie quietly for a minute or so.
- Sit or lie down comfortably, and talk your child through a guided visualization. This can be anything that feels relaxing and rejuvenating to you. You might be very specific, such as, "Picture in your mind a large grassy meadow. Feel the sun warming you. Smell the flowers. There are so many flowers, all different colors. Picture that in your mind..." Or you might present a more open-ended visualization: "Picture a place outside, somewhere you love to be, and put yourself there. Imagine exactly what it looks like and feels like to be there. Picture it as clearly as you can. Take a deep breath and smell all the wonderful smells of this beautiful place..."

❑ **Words that work**

Using affirmations can be challenging at first if you aren't used to it, but it can be very rewarding and uplifting once you get the hang of it. With your child, brainstorm a list of words or positive, life-affirming statements, and then choose a few to write down or draw into a picture. Possible affirmations include:

I feel healthy and full of energy.

This day is a blessing.

I am filled with love and joy.

I feel creative and full of good ideas.

Life is full of wonderful surprises.

This can be put on the wall or posted anywhere that it will be noticed throughout the day. Tell your child to repeat the affirmation, either silently or aloud, throughout the day. In the evening, talk about how it felt to say the affirmation, and if it had any noticeable effect on mood or attitude.

Grade 3
Mindfulness with purpose

- ❑ **Find where the feeling is**

Connecting the body to the emotions can help children to identify how emotions can manifest in the body. Understanding this process can help your child learn to release emotions. This exercise asks your child to identify where in the body a particular emotion is being felt. When your child feels sad, where is the sadness? When he or she is frustrated, where is the frustration? It's different for everyone, but it can really diffuse a strong emotion to realize that it's partially a physical sensation that can be released. The next time your child is feeling a strong emotion, encourage your child to identify the emotion and then point to where it is being felt in the body. Once the emotion is located, you might want to guide your child through a simple visualization and relaxation technique, such as the activity entitled "The energy of thought" (lesson 34) or "Breathing and visualization" in the Grade 2 activities above.

- ❑ **Lending a hand**

Using a combination of finger touches and visualization during deep breathing can help reduce anxiety and bring about a sense of quiet calm. Guide your child slowly through the following steps (both hands will be doing the same thing).

1. Sit in a comfortable position with your hands in your lap.
2. Close your eyes and touch your thumb to your index finger. Take a deep breath as you think about a time when you felt very relaxed and content.
3. Touch your thumb to your middle finger. Take a deep breath and think about how it feels to hug someone you love.
4. Touch your thumb to your ring finger and think about something you really enjoy doing.

5. Touch your thumb to your little finger and think about your favorite place to be.

This sequence of finger touches, deep breathing, and warm thoughts can be repeated several times, or just once. When your child opens his or her eyes, you might want to ask, "How do you feel?"

If this sequence seems too complicated, you can simply use the finger touches while breathing, touching the thumb to the fingers in order as you inhale to the count of four, and then touching them again in order as you exhale to the count of four.

Afterwards, ask your child to try to identify when a mindfulness technique (this one or any other) might be helpful. Would it be a good way to start or end the day? Would it be helpful to do when you are feeling stressed or unhappy about something? Would it help you relax after a busy day or after doing schoolwork? Would it help if you were feeling angry or frustrated? Once your child expresses a sense of when a mindfulness technique might be most helpful, talk about ways to help him or her remember to stop and do a technique.

❏ **Intentional living**

There are many people who strive to live an intentional life, guiding their actions, words, and thoughts in ways that intentionally support and express their core values and beliefs. Using intentional thought can benefit everyone in small ways throughout the day. For example, setting an intention for the day or for a particular project or activity can help focus your energy, your mind, and your actions. Try this exercise to introduce your child to the idea of intentional living.

When you are getting ready for your day, ask your child to name one thing that he or she intends to accomplish that day. (You might also want to include this as part of your bedtime routine, specifying one thing that you intend to do the next day.) Take a few minutes to help your child visualize how this goal or intention might unfold or come about. Ask your child to picture him- or herself successfully doing or completing this activity and to think of the steps that will lead up to it. The intention can be an external goal that has a physical element, such as completing a craft project, or a behavioral element, such as being on time for swimming lessons. Or, it can be a more internal intention, such as, "When I get scared because the neighbor's dog barks at me, I will remember that I am okay." Having this type of mindset intention is just as valid as a goal intention, and can be very helpful in developing social and emotional health and behaviors. A mindset intention could be, "I'm going to be helpful today," or "I'm going to be a good listener," or "I'm going to stand up for myself today."

Visualizing the day's intention will help it take root in your child's mind. You can also suggest that your child write it down. Perhaps a small notebook can be kept for this reason. After your child verbalizes, visualizes, and writes down the day's intention, you don't have to make any extra effort to make sure this action happens. At the end of the day, you can review the accomplishments of the day (hopefully the intended activity will be on the list) and talk about the intentions for the next day. Don't worry if unaccomplished intentions carry over to the next day—a renewed sense of motivation will make future success more likely.

Lesson 36 Unit VI Review: Whole Health

Check off the activities that have been completed in the final unit (lessons 31–35). Review topics of special interest and take some time exploring them in more detail through additional activities or further study.

Lesson 31: Active Lifestyle: Endurance

KINDERGARTEN	**Going farther than before** ❑ Counting hops ❑ Family hike ❑ Red light, green light
GRADE 1	**Healthy heart and lungs** ❑ Measuring heart rate ❑ Strong heart ❑ Belly breaths
GRADE 2	**Building stamina** ❑ Beat the clock ❑ Plus one ❑ Last year/this year/next year
GRADE 3	**Aerobic and anaerobic exercise** ❑ Which is which? ❑ Sprinting heart rate ❑ Dance party

Lesson 32: Active Lifestyle: Strength

KINDERGARTEN	**Show your muscles** ❏ Relative strength ❏ Arm wrestle ❏ Together we stand
GRADE 1	**How to grow stronger** ❏ Push yourself ❏ Crabs and frogs ❏ Be your own cheerleader
GRADE 2	**Muscle groups** ❏ Push me-pull you pairs ❏ Follow the leader ❏ The main muscle groups
GRADE 3	**Care of muscle bruises, strains, and sprains** ❏ Body check ❏ R.I.C.E. ❏ Wrap it up (mummy me)

Lesson 33: Active Lifestyle: Flexibility

KINDERGARTEN	**Stretch and bend** ❑ Twisting and turning ❑ Trees in the wind ❑ How tall? How far?
GRADE 1	**What are you stretching and why?** ❑ Muscle changes ❑ Flex and snap ❑ Before and after
GRADE 2	**Yoga** ❑ Animal poses ❑ Sun salute ❑ Balance poses
GRADE 3	**Warm up and cool down** ❑ Wiggle and flex ❑ Sweat spots ❑ After exercise

Lesson 34: Body, mind, and spirit

KINDERGARTEN	**Kindness and affirmations** ❏ Kind thoughts, kind words ❏ It's all about attitude ❏ Active relaxation
GRADE 1	**Mind and health** ❏ The energy of thought ❏ Biofeedback ❏ Following your gut
GRADE 2	**Body and spirit** ❏ Spiritual beliefs ❏ Intuition and following your path ❏ Daily reminders
GRADE 3	**Healing touch** ❏ Foot reflexology ❏ Massage ❏ Animals and touch

Lesson 35: Mindfulness and Well-being

KINDERGARTEN	**Balance and stillness** ❑ Balancing act ❑ Stillness ❑ Gratitude game
GRADE 1	**Inner awareness** ❑ At the sound of the bell ❑ One word ❑ Make your own
GRADE 2	**Deepening the connection** ❑ Inside, outside, and upside down ❑ Breathing and visualization ❑ Words that work
GRADE 3	**Mindfulness with purpose** ❑ Find where the feeling is ❑ Lending a hand ❑ Intentional living

Notes

Recommended Reading

For children

Aliki. *My Five Senses*. New York: HarperCollins, 2000. Print.

Berger, Melvin. *Why I Sneeze, Shiver, Hiccup, and Yawn*. New York: HarperCollins, 2000. Print.

Handford, Martin. *Where's Waldo?* Somerville: Candlewick, 2007. Print.

Jacques, Brian. *The Redwall Cookbook*. New York: Philomel, 2005. Print.

Kirk, Martin, Brooke Boon, and Daniel DiTuro. *Hatha Yoga Illustrated*. Champaign, IL: Human Kinetics, 2006. Print.

Leady, Loreen. *The Edible Pyramid: Good Eating Every Day*. New York: Holiday House, 2007. Print.

Pinnington, Andrea. *My Body*. New York: Scholastic, 2012. Print.

Rockwell, Lizzie. *Good Enough to Eat: A Kid's Guide to Food and Nutrition*. New York: HarperCollins, 2009. Print.

--. *The Busy Body Book: A Kid's Guide to Fitness*. New York: Knopf Boof for Young Readers, 2012. Print.

Schaefer, Valorie. *The Care and Keeping of You: The Body Book for Younger Girls*. Middleton: American Girl, 2012. Print.

Schoenberg, Joan, Steven Schoenberg, and Cynthia Fisher, illus. *My Bodyworks: Songs about Your Bones, Muscles, Heart and More!* Northampton: Crocodile Books, 2014. Print, CD.

Snel, Eline. *Sitting Still Like a Frog: Mindfulness Exercises for Kids (and Their Parents)*. Boston: Shambhala, 2013. Print.

Walter, Barbara M. and Garth Williams, illus. *The Little House Cookbook: Frontier Foods from Laura Ingalls Wilder's Classic Stories.* New York: HarperCollins, 1989. Print.

For adolescents

Gravelle, karen and Debbie Palen, illus. *The Period Book: Everything You Don't Want to Ask (But Need to Know)*. New York: Walker and Company, 2006. Print.

Gravelle, Karen, Nick Castro and Chava Castro. *What's Going on Down There? Answers to Questions Boys Find Hard to Ask*. New York: Walker and Company, 2009. Print.

Jacobs, Meredith and Sophie Jacobs. *Just Between Us: A No-Stress, No-Rules Journal for Girls and Their Moms*. San Francisco: Chronicle Books, 2010. Print.

Kapit, Wynn and Lawrence M. Elson. *The Anatomy Coloring Book*. 4th ed. New York: Pearson, 2013. Print.

Madaras, Lynda, Area Madaras, and Simon Sullivan. *The "What's Happening to My Body?" Book for Boys*. Rev. ed. New York: Newmarket Press, 2009. Print.

Madaras, Lynda and Area Madaras. *My Body, My Self for Girls (What's Happening to My Body?)*. New York: Newmarket Press, 2009. Print.

Natterson, Cara and Josee Masse, illus. *The Care and Keeping of You 2: The Body Book for Older Girls*. Middleton: American Girl, 2013. Print.

For adults

Bronson, Po and Ashley Merryman. *NurtureShock: New Thinking about Children*. New York: Hachette Book Group, 2009. Print.

ChooseMyPlate.gov. USDA. n.d. Web. 13 March 2013.

Elkind, David. *The Hurried Child: Growing Up Too Fast Too Soon*. Cambridge, MA: Perseus Books, 2001. Print.

Greenland, Susan Kaiser. *The Mindful Child: How to Help Your Kid Manage Stress and Become Happier, Kinder, and More Compassionate*. New York: Free Press, 2010. Print.

"Heritage Pyramids and Total Diet." *Oldways*. Oldways Preservation Trust. 2014. Web. 6 March 2014.

Kabat-Zinn, Myla and Jon Kabat-Zinn. *Everyday Blessings: the Inner Work of Mindful Parenting*. New York: Hyperion, 1977. Print.

Kunz, Kevin. *Reflexology: Health at your Fingertips*. New York: DK Publishing, 2003. Print.

Taylor, Kathy and Joy Drake. *The Original Angel Cards Book: Inspirational Messages and Meditations*. New York: Narada Productions, 2006. Print.